Driver and rider training from RAC

KT-494-030

Get a free driving lesson

when you book 10 lessons

Plus get a free
'map' CD-ROM

'map'
Guaranteed to improve
your chances of passing*

*Those who have used the 'map' CD-ROM had a 16% higher pass
rate in the Practical Test than those who didn't (BSM research, 2003).

BSM

the Best Start in Motoring

More value at no extra cost...

...Not only will you get your tenth lesson <u>free</u> when you book 10 lessons, but we'll also give you our award-winning 'map' Mind Alertness Programme worth £18.99 <u>free</u>.

'map' is an interactive CD package that gives you a better chance of passing your Practical Test by improving a range of mental abilities, such as judging speed and distances.

Plus, you'll also get:

– free Theory Test and Hazard Perception training

– free RAC Roadside cover when you pass

... And you can top it all off by training in one of our air-conditioned Vauxhall Corsas or Astras

So, what are you waiting for, book now

08457 276 276
www.bsm.co.uk
Quote VPYDT

Free driving lesson plus free 'map' CD-ROM
Simply present the completed coupon to your Instructor before your first lesson.

	BSM Centre use only
Name _____	Centre code _____
Address _____	PEP No. _____
_____	Value _____
Postcode _____	Car No. _____
Date _____ Mobile ____	Date _____
	Code VPYDT _____

Pass Your Driving Test

Published by BSM in association with
Virgin Books

First published in the UK in 2003 by
The British School of Motoring Ltd
1 Forest Road
Feltham
Middlesex
TW13 7RR

Second reprint 2005

ISBN 0-7535-0890-7

Design, typesetting and reprographics by Thalamus Publishing

Printed in Italy

Contents

Foreword

Driving is an enjoyable and useful lifetime experience. That is why every year nearly a million new learner drivers take to the road, each with one clear ambition. This ambition is almost certainly the same as yours – to pass their driving test first time.

Of course, there is no substitute for practical experience when learning to drive, and the best way to gain this is by taking lessons with a good professional driving instructor who uses the most up-to-date teaching techniques in a modern, dual-controlled car. However, to get the most out of your lessons it is important to prepare and this book will help you, not just to prepare for the test, but also to get the maximum value and advantage from your lessons.

Since the introduction of the Theory Test – and more recently the Hazard Perception element of the Theory Test – most people study for the Theory Test while learning to drive. The companion volumes Pass Your Driving Theory Test and Theory Test Questions are the ideal books to help you do just that. Various other training aids are also available from your local BSM Centre – check with them for details of our current range. If you are planning to practise with a friend or relative between lessons, you should recommend Practice Sessions as the book for them to study to help you.

Pass Your Driving Test has been developed to help you learn to drive more easily and enjoyably. Using a mixture of illustrations and text that talk to you just like your instructor, the book takes you through all the stages that a learner driver needs to complete before taking and passing that all-important Practical Test. And because it also gives important advice on motorway driving and on how to drive at night, or in bad weather, it will continue to be a useful

Theory Test Questions for Car Drivers

2003–2004

All the Official DSA Questions and Answers

Presented in easy-to-manage sections

the Best Start in Motoring

BSM

– Contains all the questions from the Driving Standards Authority databank, any 35 of which you may be asked in the Theory Test.

companion once you have achieved the freedom of the road.

There are no short cuts to becoming a safe and competent motorist. So, make sure you have enough experience behind the wheel and that you are fully aware of the rules of the road. Pass Your Driving Test will help you develop your driving skills and ensure that what you learn during the course of your lessons will lay the foundations for the way you drive for the rest of your life.

In over 90 years of teaching people to drive, BSM instructors have helped millions of people pass their driving test. In my view, Pass Your Driving Test is the best book available to help you make the most of your driving lessons and ensure that you approach your Practical Test in a structured and positive way.

Keith Cameron
Road Safety Adviser

Practice Sessions
A guide to accompanying the learner driver

How to be of real help
How to achieve positive practice sessions
How to be the BSM's trusted back-up

the Best Start in Motoring   BSM

– Keith Cameron is one of Britain's leading authorities on motoring and driver education. He has held a number of senior positions within the Department of Transport including Chief Driving Examiner, where he had responsibility for all UK driving tests.

– An invaluable reference and teaching aid for anyone intending to accompany a learner driver between Driving Instructor lessons.

Introduction

For most of us, learning to drive means passing the Driving Standards Agency Test. We want to achieve the freedom of travel that a full driving licence bestows. That moment when we receive our Pass Certificate and can tear up the L-plates is a time of extraordinary joy and relief.

Sadly, only about 50% of all practical driving tests conducted result in a pass, which is frustrating for candidates and examiners alike. There are as many tears of sadness as of joy. If you have started, or are about to start to learn to drive, you should recognise that this is a very important time in your life. If you want to be successful, you need to give a lot of thought as to how best to achieve your goal.

– Passing your driving test – a great moment in anyone's life.

The aim of this book is to make your life easier, by helping you to pass the test as quickly as possible, and with the minimum amount of hassle. That aim is shared by everyone at BSM, and this book is the collected wisdom and advice of many of the best current and past BSM instructors in the country.

The step-by-step approach this book uses will make it easy for you to learn, and is similar to the format used by good instructors. You will also find that your study forms an excellent preparation for the practical driving lessons and test.

Because it illustrates the habits you need to acquire to be a safe driver, the book also sets you on the right road to improving your skills after the test and surviving and remaining accident-free on today's busy roads.

Preparing for your test

As you probably know, the driving test is now split into two parts. The first is a theory test of your knowledge, attitudes and hazard perception and the second is a practical test of your driving.

This book focuses on the skills you need to master in order to pass the practical part of the Driving Test. Other publications are available from BSM to help with the Theory Test – please contact your local BSM Centre for details.

The first section of this book explains how to get started. It discusses how to

Driver faults..........3
Serious faults........0
Dangerous faults..0

PASS

obtain a licence and how to plan your lessons, as well as how to plan extra practice and study to prepare yourself for both the theory and practical parts of the Test. It will also tell you about what happens on the day of the practical Driving Test itself.

What the examiner is testing on your practical test

This book takes you step-by-step through each and every item on which you may be tested. It explains the correct way to do things, the common problems people have, and provides tips on how to improve. Examiner tips are also given, to tell you what the examiner is looking for and the typical reasons why people fail.

You need to know how examiners mark the test. Basically, there are three types

– The examiner will mark you on the three types of fault you may have committed.

of fault which you might commit during the test.

The first – known as a driver fault – is one of a minor nature. Made individually, you would not fail for these. However, if you are marked with more than 15 driver faults throughout the test, you would fail.

The second is a serious fault and the third is a dangerous fault. You will fail if you commit one serious or dangerous fault. A serious fault is one which is potentially dangerous. A dangerous fault is one involving actual danger to the candidate, examiner, the general public or property.

After the test

This section explains what happens when you pass or fail the Practical Test and gives advice on what to do next.

Driving on your own

When you have passed your test, you will still have much to learn. The last few sections of the book detail the following:

– You and your car

– Five habits that will help keep you safe when driving

– Safe night driving

– Safe motorway driving

– The look and learn method.

Many illustrations and diagrams have been used in this book to make the learning more enjoyable and to help you remember what you have learned. By studying the diagrams and their accompanying explanations, you will be able to understand easily the essential points and procedures you need to know to pass your Driving Test.

The need for a professional driving instructor

The Driving Standards Agency strongly recommends that you take lessons from an Approved Driving Instructor. There is no doubt that this is both the best and the safest way to learn.

– While the accompanying diagrams give factual information, the illustrations will help you to remember the faults you must avoid.

Any person who gives car driving lessons for payment or reward must be registered with the Driving Standards Agency. He or she is required to display an ADI identification certificate on the windscreen of the training car.

To become an ADI, you must pass examinations which are of a high standard.

Developing your driving skills

If you study this book carefully you will improve your chances of passing your Driving Test first time. You should learn more quickly, because you will better understand what your instructor explains to you.

The hope is that you will also begin a lifelong interest in developing your driving skills. Driving can be a great pleasure, but also a great risk. Skilled drivers understand both the pleasure and the risks and show by every action they take, that they care for their own and other people's safety.

One person killed or injured on our roads is one too many. In reality thousands of people's lives are ruined or ended every year by road accidents. Nearly all these deaths and injuries are the result of driver error and could be avoided. Nobody expects to have an accident and nor will you. If you care about people, you will choose to drive in a way that seeks to make your expectation a reality and you will remain accident free.

Good luck!

– Look forward to an accident-free future.

Section 1

Preparing for learning to drive

You want to learn to drive and probably can't wait to get started. You are probably excited at the prospect and, like many people, you may also feel a touch nervous about actually making a car move down the road for the first time. Don't worry about it, because all these feelings are perfectly natural.

Before you can actually sit behind the wheel, there are a few things you must do if you want to stay legal.

The legal requirements

The minimum age at which you are normally allowed to drive a car on the public roads is 17. If you are disabled and in receipt of mobility allowance, the minimum age is 16. Until the day when you pass the practical part of your Driving Test, you are not allowed to drive on your own. You must be accompanied by a person who is over 21 years of age and who has held a full British driving licence, valid for the type of vehicle you wish to drive, for a minimum of three years.

– If you are under the age you're legally allowed to drive – wish on!

Before you start to drive, you must obtain a provisional driving licence. You can get the application form D1 from any BSM Centre or from any Post Office. But sending off for your licence is not enough. You must not drive until you have received this first licence and have signed it in ink.

– Do not place L-plates in the windows where they may obstruct your vision.

Before you drive, you must also make sure that your eyesight meets the minimum standard. The next section will explain what the standard is and how you will be tested. You can test yourself by reading car numberplates from further away than the minimum distance required. You can wear glasses or contact lenses if you need to, and any optician will be pleased to give you an eye test if you are at all unsure.

You must check that any vehicle you drive is taxed. The tax disc must be displayed on the nearside (left) corner of the windscreen.

You must check that the vehicle is insured for you to learn to drive in. If it is more than three years old, check that it

has an MOT Certificate. You must fix L-plates of the regulation size to the vehicle so that they can be seen from front and rear. Do not put L-plates in the windows where they will restrict your vision.

Personal preparation

Since 1996 the Driving Test has been split into two parts; a written Theory Test of multiple-choice questions and Hazard Perception exercises, and a Practical Test of your driving. In May 1999, the Driving Test was extended to around 45 minutes and now covers more town and higher speed roads including dual carriageways where possible. You must pass both parts before you can obtain a full driving licence, and you must pass

– If your car is more than three years old, check that it has an MOT Certificate.

the Theory Test before you are allowed to apply for the Practical Test.

No two people are the same and you must decide for yourself how you wish to go about your learning for both parts of the test. Some people prefer to get the theory under their belt first, before starting driving lessons. While that is fine for some, many people find it feels too much like academic hard graft, because there is no chance to link the theory to the practice.

Most people seem to find it easier to

15

– Wear sensible shoes so that you can feel and control the pedals properly.

study theory and start driving lessons at the same time. The chance to put some of the theory into practice brings it alive and makes it feel more relevant and understandable.

Using the theory also tends to help you remember the answers to the questions without the boredom of trying to learn them parrot-fashion. Also practising Hazard Perception skills on a PC or video and then applying this knowledge on the road, will clearly enhance your skills and improve your chances of passing the tests first time.

If you study in this way at BSM, you will also receive invaluable help from your instructor, who can select from a unique range of BSM materials and learning aids designed to make learning as simple and easy as possible for every type and age

of learner. Even if you have never passed an examination in your life, or the last time you did any study was 50 years ago, with the right help you will be successful at the Theory Test. So don't worry about it, but do plan for it.

When you start to have lessons, make sure that you wear comfortable shoes. Heavy boots or high heels make it hard to feel and control the pedals.

Applying for the driving test

The purpose of the Practical Test is to find out whether you can drive safely, without supervision, on the roads. You will not pass unless you can show the examiner that you have this ability.

Most people find it best to apply for the test as soon as they have passed the theory part. This gives you a goal to aim for and encourages you to keep learning. The number of lessons and amount of practice you have each week will obviously affect how long it will take you to reach the required standard. You should discuss this with your instructor, who can then advise you about requesting an appropriate test date.

Don't be tempted to take your test before you are ready, as you will simply waste your money. You can always cancel your test appointment and book another date without losing your fee, provided you give notice of at least ten clear working days. Your driving instructor or local BSM Centre can book a test for you or give you a test application form. After booking you will receive a test appointment card. Make sure you show this card to your instructor and keep it somewhere safe.

The day of your test

Your Practical Test will last about 45 minutes. All the items on which you will be tested are covered in later sections of this book. You should bring your test appointment card and, if you are not taking your Test in a driving school car, your insurance certificate. You must also bring your driving licence and some other acceptable proof of identity that bears your name, photograph and signature.

Make sure your car is clean and in good working order.

Arrive in plenty of time. Be warned, some test centres do not have toilets. The examiner will appear, call out your name, ask you to sign against your name and also to show proof of identity. Then you will be asked to lead the way to your vehicle.

The examiner will ask you which car is yours, and then ask you to read a car numberplate. Your Practical Driving Test will have begun.

– It never hurts to make a good impression on the examiner, so make sure your car is clean and in good working order.

Eyesight Test

Advances in modern technology mean that most people, even with very severe physical disabilities, can still learn to drive and pass a Driving Test in a specially adapted car. Unfortunately, there is no such help available for the partially sighted, unless glasses or contact lenses are sufficient to solve their problem.

This is because good eyesight is essential for safe driving. You must be able to read a car numberplate from a distance of 20.5 metres (67 feet). You are allowed to wear glasses or contact lenses if necessary, but if you have any doubts about your ability to meet the eyesight requirements easily, seek advice from an optician before you start to drive or take the Test.

Most people are able to detect movement to the left and right without moving their heads. This is called your 'field of vision' and is normally 180°. Some people suffer from a severely restricted field of vision, which is referred to as 'tunnel vision'. People with tunnel vision can see only a little to the left or right without moving their heads. If you suffer from this problem, you should seek advice from an optician.

Anyway, it makes sense to have your eyesight checked regularly by an optician. The chart below shows the usual distance test, in which letters of graded sizes are viewed.

Some people are colour-blind. This disability does not stop you from driving, but you should make sure that your driving instructor is aware of your problem. Driving instructors will want to be extra sure that you can recognise road signs by their shapes and understand the sequence of lights at traffic signals and pelican crossings, as this is more difficult without the colour to help you.

– You will be asked to read a numberplate. If you fail to read it, the examiner may have to get out a tape measure to check the minimum legal distance.

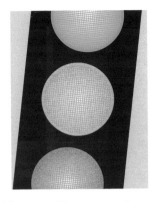

It is illegal to drive a car if you cannot pass the eyesight test.

Soon after leaving the waiting room at the beginning of your test, examiners will ask you to read a car numberplate. They will pick a distance further away than the minimum 20.5 metres. If you cannot read it, they will move closer to another plate. If you still have problems, they will use a tape measure to mark out the exact distance of 20.5 metres to another numberplate. If you still cannot read it, you will fail the test and will not be asked to drive.

Remember, if you wear glasses or contact lenses to read the numberplate, you must continue to wear them the whole of the time you are driving.

Vehicle safety questions

A new section was introduced to the Practical Test in September 2003. This is sometimes called 'show me, tell me'. Before getting into the car at the start of the Test, the examiner will ask you two

– Colour blindness could affect your understanding of traffic light sequence.

questions relating to vehicle safety and maintenance.

The intention of these oral questions is to check that drivers know how to ensure that their vehicle is safe for use. While you will be expected to open the car's bonnet, you won't be expected to have detailed mechanical knowledge. You will be asked one 'show me' and one 'tell me' question. One or both questions answered incorrectly will result in one driver fault being recorded before you have even got into the driving seat.

The topic areas for 'show me, tell me' are as follows:

Under the bonnet

How to open the bonnet, lift it and secure it

How to check the oil level against the minimum / maximum markers

How to check the engine coolant level

How to check the windscreen washer reservoir level

How to check the hydraulic brake fluid reservoir level

Inside the car

How to check that the power-assisted steering is working before starting a journey

How to check the parking brake for excessive wear

How to check the horn is working
How to check the brakes are working
before starting a journey

Lights

How to check the direction indicators
are working
How to check the brake lights are
working
How to check that the headlights and
tail lights are working

Tyres

Where to find the information for the
recommended tyre pressures
How tyre pressures should be checked
How to check tread depth on tyres
How to check that the general condition
of the tyres is roadworthy

After the eyesight check and the two
'show me, tell me' questions, the
practical drive will begin.

Examiner tips

The examiner expects you to:

– Be able to read a numberplate with
letters 79.4 mm high from a distance
of 20.5 metres (about 67 feet),
wearing glasses or contact lenses if
you need them.

– Wear your glasses or contact lenses
throughout the test if you wore them
to read the numberplate.

– Answer both the 'show me' and 'tell

me' questions correctly; you should
ensure that your driving instructor
deals fully with this area of the Test
and takes you through the answers to
possible questions as your lessons
progress.

Common problems and reasons for failure

Obviously, if you can't read the
numberplate you will fail immediately.
The distance is, after all, a minimum
requirement, and commonsense would
suggest a visit to an optician would save
a lot of time and money.

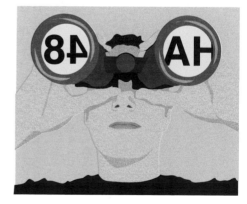

– You won't even be asked to drive if you can't
read the numberplate.

Section 2

Checks before starting the engine

While you are learning to drive you will always be climbing into a driving seat that someone else has just been sitting in. Because we all vary so much in size and build, chances are you will need to adjust the seat and mirrors in order to be safe and comfortable. This is the sequence of actions you should go through each time you get into the car. It is easily remembered as the DSSSM – this stands for Doors, Seat, Steering, Seatbelt, Mirrors. So let's take each one in turn.

Doors

Make sure your door is properly closed. You don't want it flying open as soon as you steer round the first corner. Check that all the other doors are closed as well. If you are in any doubt get out and see.

Seat

Your seat needs to be in a position so that you can reach the foot controls easily. The pedal on the left, called the clutch, goes down the furthest. Push that one to the floor and adjust the seat so that you are not stretching for it but have a slight bend in the knee, when it is pressed to the floor. Raise your foot up and down a couple of times. If your knee hits the steering wheel you can lower the seat – some cars have height adjustment – or raise the steering wheel.

Steering

You need to be able to move your hands freely around the steering wheel. Place both hands at the top of the wheel. You should have a slight bend in your elbows. If you have to stretch or are too close, you can change the angle of the back of the seat on most cars. Next, check the head restraint. This is very important as it will minimise the risk of whiplash in an accident if it is properly adjusted. The top

– Because we all differ in size and build, you may have to adjust the seat position and mirrors for every lesson.

of the head restraint should be roughly in line with the top of your ears. When taking the driving test the passenger seat must also have a head restraint.

Seatbelt

Always wear your seatbelt. This is a legal requirement. Any passengers must also belt up. If there are seatbelts in the back of the car, passengers must wear them. You are legally responsible for anyone under the age of 14 and must make them wear their seatbelts.

– This shows the view you should see in the correctly positioned driver's door mirror.

Mirrors

You have probably got three mirrors on your car. The interior one should be adjusted so that you can see as much of the rear windscreen, and therefore the road behind, as possible without having to move your head.

The door mirrors need to show a sliver of the car down the edge of the mirror and be angled so that you can see as far down the road as possible. They should be neither pointing down at the road nor up at the sky. They should show half road and half everything else.

It is probably easiest to adjust the mirrors while parked on a level road. When on test an internal mirror must be fitted for use by the examiner.

Once you have passed your test and own your own car, you may well be the only person who drives it. The seat, therefore, will always be in the correct position. The mirrors, though, ought to be checked every time. Someone could have knocked the door mirrors and you could have knocked the interior mirror. Also, some people find that they seem to settle down as the day goes on and when they get in the car in the evening their posture has changed to such an extent that the mirrors need readjusting. Strange, but this could well happen to you too.

Before you switch on the engine you must get into the habit of checking the hand brake is firmly on and the gear lever is in neutral. It is not unknown for people to have their car leap forward, into the car in front, because they had left their car in gear and forgotten to check before switching on. It is a matter of habit, and you should make these two checks part of your routine.

23

Examiner tips

The examiner will expect you to:

– Make sure all the doors are closed

– Ensure your seat and head restraint are properly adjusted

– Check your mirrors are properly adjusted

– Fasten your seatbelt.

The examiner will also be looking to see that you:

– Make sure the hand brake is on and the gear lever is in neutral.

– Check the car is not in gear before starting the engine.

Common problems and reasons for failure

The main fault seen on a driving test is starting the car in gear and it shooting forwards. It's normally a driver fault if done with no one around. However, if done repeatedly (even if there is no actual danger), it would be seen as potentially serious and a fail would result immediately. Obviously, if the fault occurred and a pedestrian was close in front (or behind if in reverse), then once would be enough for you to fail.

A popular misconception is that you have to make a great show of yanking up the hand brake and wiggling the gear lever to let the examiner see that you have checked. A quick check is sufficient.

Another misconception is that after stalling you will fail for starting in gear with the clutch depressed. Provided that it is done safely and you are able to restart and get away fairly quickly, you have made good progress and this is not a problem.

Section 3

Using the controls

You do not need to be a car mechanic to drive well, but you do need to know enough about the controls of a car to be able to operate them properly while driving. If you want or expect to get the best from your car, you need to use the controls sympathetically. A basic understanding of what you do to make a car move is, therefore, advisable. So let's take each control in turn and explain what you need to know about it.

Accelerator

The pedal on the right is called the accelerator. Instructors usually refer to it as the 'gas pedal', simply because it is quicker to instruct 'More gas' than it is to say, 'Press the accelerator down a little further'.

It is operated by the right foot and controls the speed of the car. The further down you press it, the faster the engine runs, which in turn drives the car's wheels faster. When you ease off the gas pedal the engine runs more slowly and the car slows down. It is a very sensitive pedal, only slight pressure is required to get a result. You need to be able to operate this control smoothly, and it is probably best to rest your heel on the floor and just use the ball of your foot and toes to work the pedal.

– The accelerator is often called the 'gas pedal', after gasolene (petrol).

Foot brake

The middle pedal is the foot brake. It is also only operated with your right foot because there is usually no need to be speeding the car up while simultaneously slowing it down. The foot brake works on all four wheels of the car. Don't stamp on this pedal but squeeze it progressively until the car comes to a stop and, as it does so, ease off the pedal to avoid a jolt. When you touch the brake, two red 'brakelights' come on at the back of the car, informing other road users that you are slowing down.

Clutch

The pedal on the left is the clutch. It is operated with the left foot and is used to move the car away, to change gear and to stop the car without stalling the engine. Without a basic understanding of what is happening to the car when you use the clutch, you won't know what it does. Think back to when you were a passenger in a car. Picture the driver stopping the car at red lights. The engine keeps running, doesn't it? This is because the driver puts the clutch down as the car comes to a stop and in doing so, disconnects the engine from the wheels. Thus the clutch enables the wheels of the car to stop turning without the engine cutting out.

Now, picture the lights turning to green. The driver selects another gear and the car simply appears to move away. But it is not so simple: the car moves because the driver has raised the clutch, enabling the engine to drive the wheels. Because

you are operating the clutch against a strong spring, you need to raise the clutch slowly and smoothly. At the point at which the car starts to move – often referred to as the 'biting point' – you need to keep your feet still to allow the car to move away smoothly and under control. As soon as the car is moving you can raise the clutch fully.

You should avoid resting your foot on the clutch when it is not in use, because this causes unnecessary wear and tear on the mechanism.

Gears

The gear lever is always operated together with the clutch. The gears are used to match the speed of the engine to the speed of the car. As the car picks up speed you need to select a higher gear. Each gear has a limited amount of power; the higher the gear, the less the power, but the more the speed.

– When raising the clutch, the point at which the car starts to move is referred to as the 'biting point'.

Imagine having to push a car out of the way because it has run out of petrol. You need an enormous amount of power and effort to get this cumbersome lump of metal moving. As soon as you have some momentum, it takes far less effort to keep it rolling. Similarly in driving, in order to get the car moving you need the gear with the most power, which is the first gear. Once the car is moving you can change up to second and so on through the gears until the car is at the top speed for the conditions.

Slowing down is the same. You need to match the gear to the speed of the car, so that when you come to accelerate again the car has the right amount of power to go.

– Don't look down at the gear lever when changing gears.

Hand brake

The hand brake is used to secure the car once it has stopped. Normally, it only works on the car's back. To apply it, you push the button in and pull it up. Pushing the button in cuts out the irritating clicking noise or the ratchet and prolongs the hand brake's life.

To release the hand brake, pull it up slightly and push the button in, then drop the lever to the floor.

Steering

Steering a steady course along the road has much to do with how you use your eyes. Don't look down at the end of the bonnet, because this tends to make you weave from one side of the road to the other.

Looking well ahead helps keep the car in a straight line. So keep your head up and your eyes high.

Keep both hands on the steering wheel. Position them at ten-to-two, or a quarter-to-three.

Remember, it is normally only the front wheels that steer. When you turn left, the back wheels cut in and will mount the kerb if you steer too early.

When turning right, you will cut the corner if you steer too early.

It is not always necessary to go up and down through the gears in order. It is often better to skip a gear in order to match the speed of the engine to the road speed. Brakes are for slowing and gears are for going. This means that if you are in fourth or fifth gear and need to stop at red lights, you brake to a stop and then select first gear to go.

You need to practise moving the gear lever into the various positions, because when you are driving you should keep your eyes on the road ahead when changing gear.

Ancillary controls

You need to familiarise yourself with all the minor controls of the car. The indicators can be found on either the left or the right of the steering wheel. Know where your lights are and how to operate the windscreen wipers, demisters and heaters.

Examiner tips

The examiner will expect you to:

– Use all the controls smoothly and correctly

– Understand the function of the main and ancillary controls.

The examiner will also be looking to see that you:

– Balance the accelerator and clutch to move away smoothly

– Accelerate evenly

– Avoid stalling the car

– Choose the right gear and change in good time before a hazard

– Brake gently and in good time

– Know how and when to apply the hand brake

– Hold the steering wheel at either the ten-to-two or quarter-to-three position

– Steer at the correct time and smoothly

– Understand the minor controls, such as lights, indicators, windscreen wipers and de-misters

– Know the meaning of displays on the instrument panel, such as warning lights and speedometer.

Common problems and reasons for failure

Accelerator, clutch:
– Lack of co-ordination

– Foot resting on clutch

– Stalling

– Jerky acceleration.

Gears:
– Wrong gear for speed and conditions

– Leaving gear change too late, so getting into a hazard situation and having to steer round it and change gear all at the same time

– Coasting – this is marked as a gear fault, not a clutch fault

– Examiners like to see block changing, but single changing would not be regarded as a fault, provided it was done correctly

– You should assess the corner and

29

select the appropriate gear, rather than automatically selecting second

– Normally changing into the wrong gear on odd occasions would be a driver fault unless it was a shattering experience, like fourth to first gear at 40mph.

Brakes:

Harsh use and late braking is not normally a failure unless it happens every time. But remember that more than 15 driver faults in the test means failure.

Hand brake:

– Leaving it on when travelling

– Using it to stop

– Not using the ratchet button – this is more an irritation than a driving fault.

Steering:

Position of hands is not rigidly enforced in these enlightened days, but if you are tying your arms in knots this will result in failure

If you constantly cross hands it would cause the examiner to look very closely at your line and accuracy of steering.

– When steering, tying your arms in knots will result in a fail.

Section 4   Moving off

Now that you know all about the controls of the car, you need to know how to use them to get the car moving. For some, the biggest nightmare is that you might kangaroo-hop down the road. That you might do this, or stall, the first time you move away may well be your greatest dread. But it is actually insignificant in comparison to being safe. And anyway, with a good instructor you should be able to move the car smoothly, even the first time you attempt it. The crucial thing is that you can move away without endangering or annoying other road users.

Safety first

First, an explanation of how to ensure your safety when you move away; then what you need to do to move away smoothly and under control.

Once you have the car prepared and ready to move, you need to look for a safe gap. This means a gap that is big enough for you to pull into without causing any other road user to slow down, swerve or stop.

You do this by looking in your mirrors, especially the interior and right-door mirrors. If the road behind looks reasonably clear, have a look over your right shoulder into the area not covered by your mirrors – the 'blindspot'. You are looking for vehicles, cyclists or pedestrians coming out of driveways or trying to cross the road. You also need to check the road ahead, making sure that oncoming vehicles aren't on your half of the road. Keep looking all around.

This is all part of a routine called Mirror, Signal, Manoeuvre, or MSM.

The manoeuvre part is any change of direction or change of speed. In moving off you are changing both direction and speed, so you need to use the MSM routine. Having checked your mirrors, blindspots and the road ahead, you should decide on a signal.

Give a signal if it would help another road user.

Before you move, have a final check all around, including the blindspot, to make sure that it is still safe.

The situation can change very quickly, especially when you are new to it all. Don't be afraid to take your time at first. The observations are extremely important. With practice you will be able to look for, and decide on, a safe gap much quicker.

Having considered how to move away safely, you now need to know how to

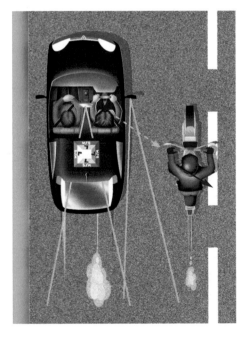

– You won't see objects in your interior and right-door mirror blindspots, so look over your shoulder as well.

– When moving off uphill, press the accelerator harder than you would to get away on a level road.

move away under control. You need to be able to do this on a level road, on a gradient and from behind a parked car. Each situation requires varying degrees of control.

You must select the appropriate gear and co-ordinate the relevant controls to keep the car stationary while you see if it is safe to move.

If you are on a level road:
– Put the car in first gear

– Press your foot gently on the accelerator pedal

– Let the clutch out slowly to the biting point

– Release the hand brake and let the car creep forwards

– Let the clutch up smoothly and all the way

– Steer to a normal driving position, generally a metre from the kerb.

If you are facing uphill:
– Put the car in first gear

– Press the accelerator pedal a bit harder than you would on the level, the engine has more work to do, so it needs more power

– Let the clutch out slowly to the biting point and release the hand brake

33

– Keep the car stationary or let it move forwards slightly. Do not let it roll backwards. Do not jerk or allow the car to stall. Keep pressure on the gas pedal as you let the clutch out smoothly all the way. Do not race the engine.

If you are facing downhill:

– Put the car in first gear (if the hill is very steep use a higher gear)

– Apply the foot brake

– Release the hand brake

– If you are moving away from behind a parked vehicle, you will need to use clutch control in order to move slowly until you can see it is safe to pull out.

– Release the foot brake slowly. As the car starts to roll forwards, release the clutch smoothly and fully and press the accelerator gently.

Moving away at an angle

If another car is parked close to your car, you may have to move off at a sharp angle. This procedure is similar to pulling away in a straight line, but you may need to move very slowly in order to give yourself time to steer. You do this by using what is called 'clutch control'. You keep the gas at an even rate and, as you let the clutch pedal up to the biting point, the car will start to move. A slight pressure on the clutch pedal will slow you down or bring the car to a stop again. Ease the clutch up a fraction and you will creep forwards again. In this way, you can creep forwards or backwards a few inches at a time whenever you are in a confined space or need to edge forwards to see clearly.

But remember:

– Use the clutch to keep the car creeping forwards slowly or to hold it still if necessary

– Turn the steering wheel much more, first to the right, then to the left

– Be very observant and extra careful – look behind several times as you move away to make sure it is still safe

– Check the road ahead more carefully. If the road is narrow, you may block the path of any oncoming traffic.

You will probably be asked to carry out these exercises on your driving test. But if you have to move away around a parked vehicle from the Test Centre, or emerge from a junction on an up or downhill gradient right at the start, the examiner will assess your ability to control the car at the time. In which case he won't specifically ask you to do these exercises separately.

Now you need to know how to stop the car before you have a go at moving away.

As you are driving along, look for a safe place to stop. You will probably be on a fairly quiet road, but there are obvious places to avoid. Don't park over someone's driveway, close to a junction or opposite another parked car if you think this would narrow the road so much that it would inconvenience others. Once you have spotted somewhere to pull up, you need to use the MSM routine. Check your interior and left-door mirrors.

You need to decide whether a signal is necessary. Start to slow the car down. Steer towards the kerb, trying to get the car as close as you can without clipping it. Once you're happy with the position, push the clutch down as you gently brake to a stop. Apply the hand brake, select neutral, cancel the signal if it is on and rest your feet. Switch off the engine if you are leaving the car.

It is probably best to practise moving off, driving a short distance, say 20 metres, and parking. Practise it with your instructor a few times until you feel happy with the controls and the safety aspect. This is what examiners have to say about moving off:

Examiner tips

The examiner will expect you to:

– Move off safely and under control on a level road, from behind a parked vehicle and on a gradient, where practical.

The examiner will also be looking to see that you:

– Use the MSM routine

– Check your blindspot for traffic and pedestrians

– Make balanced use of the accelerator, clutch, brakes and steering

– Use the appropriate gear.

Common problems and reasons for failure

You look, but do it all far too early and only then get ready to move. The check should be immediately prior to moving.

Lack of a shoulder check would be a driver fault if done only once or twice, unless you are being overtaken. Any regular miss would be classed as a pattern of driving, and a fail.

On the flat, lurching forwards and stalling an odd time would normally be a driver fault. However, if a correct move off was more a case of good luck than good management, you would almost certainly fail immediately.

On a gradient, a slight roll back would be a driver fault provided you regained control and set off smoothly.

A roll back followed by a leap skywards would generally be a serious fault.

Moving off at an angle, forgetting to check the road ahead and pulling straight into the path of an oncoming car would be a serious fault.

Having got the car moving, letting the clutch right out and lurching forwards before steering around a parked car would be a serious fault.

Not hanging on to the last bit of clutch to gain a smooth start – usually the 'biting point' – then letting it go, making a jerky start or even a stall, would be a driver fault. Remember the 15-fault threshold.

Pass Your Driving Test

The emergency stop

One of the most crucial skills you could possibly learn and develop is how to stop the car in an emergency. In an ideal world you should never have to use this skill. If you look very carefully and anticipate all the hazards on the road ahead, you should never have to stop in an emergency. But the unexpected can happen. Most emergency stops occur when a driver fails to see a danger far enough ahead and does not have the opportunity to reduce their speed in good time.

Making an emergency stop

The driving test frequently includes an exercise which is a simulation of a real emergency. The examiner will stop you at the side of the road, and it will be explained that you will shortly need to carry out an emergency stop. This usually happens near the beginning of the test.

The signal the examiner will give to tell you when to stop will be demonstrated. You will probably have it explained that you should imagine that a child has run out into the road in front of you.

Your main aim should be to stop promptly in the shortest possible distance without losing control of the car. The 'promptly' bit is probably the most important thing. Your ability to react quickly to a signal is actually what is being tested. The examiner is then in a position to gauge your ability to react quickly to a real-life emergency situation. Reacting means moving your foot off the gas pedal and onto the brake as quickly as possible.

— The examiner will demonstrate the signal he will use to tell you to make your emergency stop.

It needs to become a reflex rather than something you consciously think about. This is because what is happening in front of you is far more important than what might happen behind you. There is no need to check your mirror before braking, as the examiner will have already checked before giving the signal, because in the real world, if a child has run out in front of you, you must stop. Grip the wheel firmly with both hands.

This helps you keep the car under control and also acts as a brace, preventing you from being thrown forwards as you stop.

The braking can be quite difficult to get the hang of. It's certainly difficult to explain, but easier to practise. Basically, you brake in exactly the same way as you would do normally, except a lot more firmly. Using the ball of your foot and your toes, squeeze the pedal. Just before

– What's in front is more important, so there's
no need to check the mirror.

the car stops push down the clutch. It is best not to allow the car to stall, as you may need to move away again quickly to prevent someone from behind going into the back of you. If you push the clutch down too early you stop the engine from

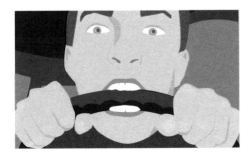

– Grip the steering wheel firmly.

assisting the braking and you increase the risk of losing control of the car.

When you have stopped, make the car safe by putting on the hand brake and selecting neutral. You are likely to have stopped in the middle of the road. Check mirrors and blindspots on both sides of the car before pulling away.

Skid control

Before leaving this subject, you need to know about skid control and prevention. If you stamp on the foot brake too fiercely you risk locking the wheels of the car and causing a skid. Prevention is better than cure, so always try to brake progressively and firmly in the first place. Should you, however, lock the wheels, you will recognise this from the screeching noise the tyres make on the road surface. Release the brake immediately and then reapply it as soon as the wheels have started turning again. If you don't release the brake quickly enough, you may feel the back end of the car sliding to the left or the right. Steer into the direction of the skid so, if the back end is moving to the right, steer right to bring it back in line. Only turn the wheel slightly because you don't want to cause a skid in the opposite direction. If you do feel the car skidding, try not to panic. Get your foot off the brake as quickly as possible.

39

Examiner tips

The examiner will expect you to:

– Stop the car promptly

– Keep the car under control without locking the wheels.

The examiner will also be looking to see that you:

– Stop the car in the shortest possible distance

– Stop the car without endangering other road users.

Common problems and reasons for failure

You should brake firmly, but avoid then letting the brake off so that you don't actually stop.

A common fault is to miss the brake pedal altogether, hit the accelerator

– If you lock the wheels when braking, you'll recognise this from the screeching noise the tyres will make.

instead and press it hard to the floor – you can imagine the examiner's lurching stomach and understand that you will fail.

If a skid just starts and you have the presence of mind to ease off and reapply the correct pressure, you may well get away with a minor fault.

A common fault is braking too hard on wet or greasy roads and then keeping the brakes on, making things worse.

There is often a move-off fault after the emergency stop because you either lurch forwards or fail to look before moving off again. Take a second to collect your thoughts and then remember everything about moving off safely and under control.

Section 6

Road junctions, including roundabouts

Once you have moved away, changed gear and stopped a few times, you will probably be eager to know how to get off the road you are on and on to another one. This next section is huge, but if you take it one step at a time you won't find it nearly as daunting as you might think.

This section deals with left and right turns first, then emerging, followed by crossroads and, finally, roundabouts. First, however, you must understand about priorities.

Priorities at road junctions

Because traffic meets at junctions, it is necessary to have rules that allow everyone to proceed safely while maintaining the best possible traffic flow.

To achieve this, traffic from a particular direction is given priority; that is, allowed to proceed first if it is safe to do so. At many busy junctions, traffic lights change the priority from one direction to another. At other junctions, the vehicles on one road always have priority over the vehicles on another. Road signs and markings are provided to tell you who has priority:

– At a Stop sign you do not have priority. You must stop and give way until it is safe for you to proceed

– At a Give Way sign you do not have priority. You must give way and stop when necessary in order to give priority to other drivers

– At unmarked junctions there are no road signs or markings and all vehicles have equal priority. Take great care.

You need to know how to turn safely from the road you are on into a side road that may be either to the left or the right.

Up until this point you will have been making use of the Mirror Signal Manoeuvre routine (MSM). We use this routine at all junctions, but to make it simpler to put into practice, the Manoeuvre is now broken down into three easy stages: Position, Speed and Look.

The first thing you need to do when driving along is identify the road into which you wish to turn. You should be able to look for clues. There may be advanced warning with a sign. You might be able to see traffic emerging or turning into the road. You can look for gaps in the buildings or between parked cars.

– At a Stop sign, stop and wait until it's safe to proceed.

Once you have located the junction, and while you are assessing it, you need to start putting the routine (MSPSL) into practice. Imagine that you are going to make a left turn from a major road into a minor road.

Mirrors

Check behind in your mirrors to see the position of any following cars, motorcyclists or pedal cyclists. At this stage you are looking to see if it is going to be safe to give your signal.

Signal

Give this in good time.

Position

Remain in your normal driving position, about a metre from the kerb. The position of your car acts as a signal and confirms to other road users that you do not in fact intend parking on the left before the junction. Try to maintain this position throughout the turn.

Speed

This needs to be at its lowest just before the turn, with the correct gear selected. In order to do this you need to start slowing the car down with the foot brake early. The less you can see into the new road, the slower you need to go. If there are any problems round the corner, such as parked cars or children playing in the road, you will then be able to stop the car safely. Often second gear will match the speed at which you need to take the turn. Select second gear approximately

– The less you can see into the new road, the slower you need to go.

two car lengths from the turn because this will give you plenty of time to raise the clutch. Maintain this speed with either the gas on a level road or travelling uphill, or the foot brake if you are travelling downhill.

Look

Check your mirrors again, especially the left-door one. Check the road ahead to see if anyone is waiting to turn right into the same road. Check into the new road for any problems you may need to deal with, and also because this will help you to determine when to start steering.

Once you have turned into the new road, check behind. If safe, gently accelerate.

Turning right

When turning right into a side road you use the same routine (MSPSL):

Mirrors

Particularly the right-door mirror. Look especially for motorbikes or cars that might be about to overtake.

Signal

Give this in good time.

Position

Steer the car over to the right slightly and position it so that it is as close to the left of the centre of the road as it is safe to be. Again, your position confirms to other road users what your signal is indicating – that you intend to turn right. If there are obstructions on the right-hand side of the road, you may need to delay your positioning.

Speed

If the road ahead is clear, your speed will be similar to the left turn. You need to be slowing down early so that you can look and assess how safe it is to make the turn.

Look

You now have to cross the path of oncoming traffic. You have two options: to go or to stop.

Go

If the road ahead is obviously clear, check behind to make sure there is nothing about to overtake, and then look

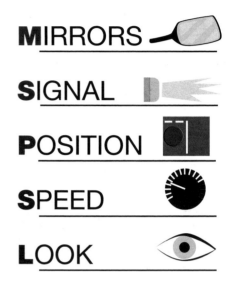

MIRRORS

SIGNAL

POSITION

SPEED

LOOK

into the new road. You are looking for any parked cars or pedestrians crossing the road. Look especially for motorbikes or cars that might be about to overtake. If there are, don't start the turn. You are also looking to identify the point at which you need to start turning the wheel. You should turn into the road and finish in the normal driving position – about a metre from the kerb – without cutting the corner or clipping the kerb.

Stop

If there is traffic coming towards you – or if you are in any doubt as to how safe it would be to make the turn – then don't make it. Wait and try to judge a safe gap so that you can turn without causing any other road user to slow down, swerve or stop. If you think you would have enough time to walk across the road, this is the same amount of time you would need to drive across the road. If you practise this a few times it eventually becomes a split-second judgement where you decide, 'yes, I could walk across the road, so therefore I will drive across'; or, 'no, there would not be enough time to walk safely across the road, so I will wait.'

– The time it would take you to walk across the road is the same time you would need to drive across the road.

Emerging onto a larger road
As you approach the end of a road, start assessing it and noticing the road markings, if there are any. Try to decide whether you could class the junction as:

Open
You have a good view into both sides of the new road; or

Closed
You can see very little of the new road into which you wish to emerge.

Open
If you have a brilliant view into the new road and you can see that there is no other traffic around, you can make your decision to emerge far sooner than if the view into the new road were restricted – provided, of course, that there isn't a Stop sign. Your speed would then depend on the control you would need in order to steer into the new road safely and smoothly.

Closed
If your view into the new road is virtually nil, you need to be prepared to slow down and even stop in order to look and emerge safely into a gap.

Whatever the visibility on the approach, you still need to make full use of the MSPSL sequence.

Start the sequence early to give yourself plenty of time to slow the car down and assess the junction.

Once you reach a point from where you can see into the new road, start looking for a safe gap. It is important that you take a good look in both directions. You need to look right to see what the situation is, and to try to assess the speed of any approaching traffic.

In the case of a left turn you need to know whether there are any obstructions or whether any traffic is overtaking and on your half of the road.

You need to look right again to check what you saw the first time.

The situation can change very rapidly and if it was safe to emerge the first time you looked, you simply need to be certain that this is still the case.

If you can't see, edge forwards. Keep your head moving all the time.

In looking, you are also checking that once you do emerge, you can do so without causing any other driver to slow down, swerve or stop. This may mean

that you need to pick your speed up rapidly to merge safely with the rest of the traffic.

Crossroads

Crossroads are often referred to as 'accident blackspots' because there are many points from which another vehicle can suddenly emerge. Therefore they need to be treated with caution.

There are two main types: marked or unmarked. Let's deal with marked crossroads first and imagine you are approaching on the main priority road with the intention of travelling straight ahead. The first thing you need to do is to recognise that you are approaching a crossroads and you do this by looking for clues in the same way as you would do if you were approaching any other junction. This time, however, you obviously need to identify two roads opposite each other.

– Check a second time before emerging – the situation can change very rapidly.

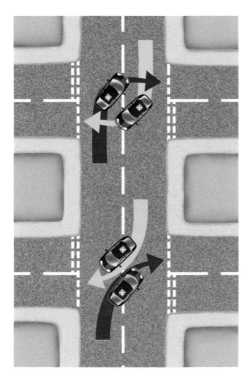

– Top: offside-to-offside passing.
  Bottom: nearside-to-nearside passing.

you can clearly see the ends of the roads you are about to pass. If there are vehicles waiting to emerge, make sure they have seen you and are not going to pull out in front of you.

In practice, your speed may actually only need to be slightly reduced before you can suitably assess that the junction is safe to travel through.

At traffic lights – where the lights have turned to green and you have moved forward to take up a position to turn right – once there is a gap in the oncoming traffic, you may find there is a vehicle opposite also wishing to turn right. There are two ways of doing this, both of which are acceptable.

Offside-to-offside

Drive slowly, moving forwards in a straight line so that you pass the other driver on your offside, or driver's side. Stop when you are almost opposite your point of turn. This is safest because from this position you have a clear view of the road ahead.

Nearside-to-nearside

Drive slowly forwards and start to steer to the right slightly so that you pass the other driver on your nearside, or passenger's side. Again, stop when you are almost opposite your point of turn. From this position your view of the oncoming traffic may be obscured by the vehicle opposite you, so take care to make sure it is safe to complete the turn.

Check for the position of any following vehicles and consider any signal you might need to give. As you are planning to travel straight ahead you will not need to indicate, so your signal might be the brake lights to warn other vehicles that you are slowing down.

Then you should match your speed to what you can see. Basically, you keep braking until you can see that it is safe to proceed. It becomes safe to go on when

47

Your decision as to whether to turn offside-to-offside or nearside-to-nearside will depend on three things:

1. The layout of the junction:

    If the crossroads is square, or your exit is further away from you than the opposite exit, you will find turning offside-to-offside to be the most convenient.

2. The road markings:

    These may dictate to you – with arrows and boxes painted on the road – where you should position your vehicle.

3. The other driver:

    Try to establish eye contact with the other driver. If, as they start to edge forwards, they keep the wheels of the car straight you will be turning offside-to-offside. If they turn the wheels to the right, you will probably be turning nearside-to-nearside. Follow suit, if it is safe to do so. If they appear to be doing the same as you, and waiting for your lead, position the car as you feel safest, taking into consideration the layout of the junction and any road markings.

Now imagine that you are approaching the crossroads with a Give Way line across your road. Your only new consideration is the road opposite.

Where there is a vehicle waiting to emerge from the road opposite, you need to strike a balance between making progress and being courteous. Try to make eye contact with the driver of the vehicle opposite, and be prepared to give way if it looks like they are about to move. There is no priority, since you are both emerging from a minor onto a major road.

When approaching a crossroads on a housing estate or country lane, you may notice that there are no road markings. This is an unmarked crossroads and needs to be treated with extreme caution. It is perfectly possible for someone who is approaching the crossroads from your right or your left to assume that they have priority over you and to keep travelling straight through the junction.

Your speed will therefore depend on what you can or cannot see. You will need to imagine a give way line and to approach the junction as if you were emerging.

Traffic roundabouts

Finally roundabouts. Roundabouts are designed to help keep everyone moving by mixing together several streams of traffic. Give way to traffic on the roundabout approaching from your immediate right.

Do not stop if it is safe to keep moving. Signal and position your car correctly for the exit you wish to take.

If you are taking the first exit on the left:

– Approach in the left-hand lane

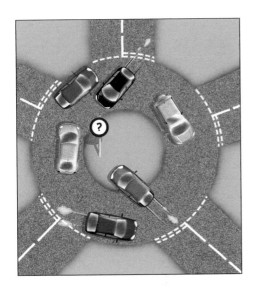

– Traffic already on the roundabout has priority, and you must give way to it.

– Signal left

– Keep to the left.

If you are going straight ahead:

– Approach in the left-hand lane

– Do not signal on approach

– Keep in the left-hand lane .

– Signal left as you pass the exit before the one you want.

If you are taking an exit to the right:

– Signal right

– Approach in the right-hand lane

– Keep to the right and continue to signal right

– As you pass the exit before the one you want, cancel signal, check mirrors and left blindspot, signal left

– Leave by the left-hand lane of the exit road unless it is blocked.

Once you know the basic rules – the MSPSL and so on – it is a case of adapting this to the particular type of junction you are approaching. The secret of success lies in the speed. Get your speed right on the approach – and that usually means really slow, really early – and you will find that everything else falls into place.

In the early stages, the slower you go, the easier you will find it. As your ability and experience grow, there will be plenty of opportunity to match your speed to the situation.

Examiner tips

The examiner will expect you to:

– Use the MSM routine

– Position correctly and adjust your speed

– Choose the correct lane where there are lane markings and in a one-way street

– Watch out for motorcyclists, cyclists and pedestrians

– Take effective observations.

The examiner will also be looking to see that you:

– Read Stop signs, Give Way signs, etc, accurately

– Assess the speed of traffic, particularly at roundabouts and when emerging.

Common problems and reasons for failure

Speed and observation are often marked together. If, for instance, you did not see an unmarked crossroads and flew across at speed without a glance in either direction, you would fail.

Observation is often done too slowly – the head is moved at such a speed that something can appear while the head is turned the wrong way.

Sticking slavishly to the 'Right-Left-Right' no matter what the junction is like. Not assessing the junction and seeing what advance observation is possible.

Not edging the vehicle forwards in order to have better vision.

Position before turning right – either you do not move to the centre of the road on a wide road and finish up blocking following traffic, or you go past the centre line, causing oncoming traffic problems. This nearly always happens where there is no white line. The degree of fault depends on how much traffic is inconvenienced.

On a narrow road at a T-junction, you insist on going to the centre of the road, causing problems for traffic turning into the junction.

One of the worst faults is moving out to the centre of a wide road, then, at the last minute, swinging back to the left, before going right around the corner. Often there is traffic overtaking on the left. A fault like this will always result in a failure.

Position before turning left – the usual fault is swinging out to the right before turning left. The degree of the fault will depend on how big a swing and whether any other vehicle is inconvenienced.

The other extreme is not allowing sufficient room and going over the kerb. Obviously if there are any pedestrians about, this is a fail. If it is blatantly obvious that you haven't a clue where the wheels are, it would be a fail. An odd brush of the kerb would be a driver fault.

Section 7

Using the mirrors

Any mention of mirrors so far has always been in a specific context, such as checking behind you on the approach to a junction or before moving away again after the emergency stop. This section takes mirrors as a subject in their own right and will help you to understand the reasons for looking behind.

Looking behind you

Whenever you are driving you need to know as much about what is happening on the road behind you as you do about what is taking place in front.

This is because the situation behind can change very quickly; and that means you must look in your mirrors frequently and always be aware of what may be in your blindspots.

– Using your mirrors well is the key to making you a good driver.

What is happening behind you can so easily affect what is happening up ahead. Until you have gathered all the information you cannot make a safe decision as to the action you might need to take. Using your mirrors well is the key to making you a good driver. It forces you out of automatic pilot mode, keeps you aware and conscious, and actually makes driving interesting and challenging because you are totally in control of the situation.

But just looking is not enough; you must also act sensibly and safely on what you see. That is what examiners are looking for when you take your driving test. They are trained to spot your eye movements, but they will pay most attention to whether your actions after you look are safe and sensible.

For example, if you move out around a parked car when another driver is overtaking you it makes little difference how many times you move your eyes towards your mirrors. You should not move out until the overtaking vehicle has passed you.

You must always use your mirrors before doing anything which might affect other road users, such as:

– Signalling

– Changing direction

– Turning left or right

– Overtaking or changing lanes

– Stopping or slowing down

– Increasing speed

– Opening your car door.

It is important to understand the reasons why you have to check your mirrors at these times, so here are some examples:

— Always check your mirrors before opening
the car door to get out.

Imagine that you wish to take the next
road on the right. You know that's where
you want to go, so you put your signal on
to make sure everyone else also knows.
What you haven't noticed is the
motorbike coming up behind, obviously
about to overtake you. Now you are
probably not going to move the car over
to the right just yet, so you perhaps don't
feel this is a problem.

The motorcyclist feels you probably
haven't seen him, which is true, and now
he has to cut back in to the left, which
may have serious consequences if there
is another vehicle following you. In other
words, you are checking your mirrors,
and especially the appropriate door
mirror, to see if it is safe to signal now or
whether it would be safer to delay the
signal until the motorbike has overtaken
you. The mirrors help you decide on the
timing of the signal.

If there is a junction ahead of
you and the lights change to
red you have to stop.

But what is the point of
checking your mirrors before
braking? If you looked well
ahead for the need to slow
down or stop, you would spot
the lights early. You could
look in your mirrors, see the
car travelling too close
behind, and start braking early, thus
spreading your braking over a longer
distance. Your brake lights would give a
warning signal to the driver behind,
allowing them plenty of time to slow
down and prevent them from hitting you.
As with checking your mirrors before
signalling, checking your mirrors before
braking is to help you decide on the
timing of your signal.

A driver may be overtaking on a dual
carriageway. Look for slow-moving cars
ahead. You will have to change to the
right-hand lane to get past. You need to
ask yourself whether it is safe to move
out; and, if a car is overtaking, whether it
will be safe after that. If it is, you need to
signal because the car behind may also
try to overtake. If you have been using
your mirrors regularly, you will already
know the answers to these questions.
A quick check before you act, to confirm
them, is all you need. If you haven't been
using your mirrors you will not have
enough time to make sufficient checks to
be certain of any of the answers.

53

It is easier to know what is happening all the time and just to confirm it when a problem arises, than it is to wait for the problem to crop up and try to get all the information you need quickly. One way lies confidence, and the other way lies hesitancy and the taking of risks.

Watch out for cars and pedestrians close by when you park. Look before you open your car doors and wait, if necessary, until it is safe.

Remember, you cannot make sensible decisions without information. To get the information, you must look – and that includes in your mirrors.

– Check mirrors before signalling – you may not have noticed someone overtaking you.

Examiner tips

The examiner will expect you to:

– Use your mirrors effectively before any manoeuvre.

The examiner will also be looking to see that you:

– Act sensibly and safely on what you see.

Common problems and reasons for failure

A common misconception is that the interior mirror should be set in such a way that you have to lean over to use it, ensuring the examiner can see you looking. You are likely to fail for not making proper use of the steering.

If you're too busy leaning over to look in the mirror, you pull the steering with you and finish up all over the road.

Another misconception is that if the examiner is not carefully watching, he cannot see whether you are using the mirror or not. False. It is very easy to watch unobtrusively.

Another erroneous belief is that any look in the mirror has to be of long duration. Gazing in the mirror too long may cause you to run into the back of a parked car.

The criteria for failure depends largely on what is around at the time the mirror is missed. An odd miss when no one is inconvenienced would be a driver fault. On a busy dual carriageway when changing lanes, one miss would make the examiner very uncomfortable and two could spell a failure. One miss with a vehicle overtaking would be a failure.

Section 8

Giving signals

The best way of getting into a heated debate with somebody about driving is to ask them whether or not they signal at a roundabout. This is because everyone seems to have their own opinion on the use of signals. It is a grey area and, once you know the rules, you have to use your commonsense and good judgement to apply them.

The point of signalling

Signals are the language of driving. They warn other road users that we are there, or that we intend to change speed or direction in some way.

To be of any use, it is important that:

– Everyone understands what they mean. For this reason you should only use the signals shown in the Highway Code

– They are given early and clearly enough for others to see them and respond to them

– They are not misleading or confusing.

Signals can be given in a variety of ways: direction indicators; arm signals; brake lights; horn; headlights; reversing lights.

On your driving test, your examiner will expect you to signal in plenty of time

– To avoid confusion, only give signals shown in the Highway Code.

whenever it would help another road user. In busy towns, you will nearly always need to give a signal when turning left or right.

But remember that there is no point in giving a signal if there is no one who could benefit from it. For example, if you are moving off from the side of the road and the street is deserted, you should not signal. This will also help show the examiner that you are thinking about what you see.

You should always check your mirrors first so that you can decide whether it is safe to give a signal. Remember that

– Do not give confusing signals.

Do not give confusing signals. For example, imagine giving a signal to pass a parked car where there is a junction on the right. A driver waiting to emerge from the right may see the signal and suppose that you are turning right. The driver may also presume that you will be slowing down to make the turn and that there will be enough time to slip out. Of course, you're not going to be slowing down and all you will see is a car pulling out of a road on the right directly in front of you. In this example you can see that the signal to pass the parked car was misleading. You could move out earlier and so signal your intentions with the position of your car.

Do not signal too early. If there are two side roads close together, a signal given too soon may make people think you are going to turn before you actually do.

Time your signal carefully if you intend to stop on the left. If you are stopping just beyond a junction, do not signal until you pass it. Otherwise, a driver waiting to emerge may think you are turning left and pull out in front of you.

Do not signal too late. If you suddenly decide that the road on the right is the road you wish to take, don't brake, signal right and cut across oncoming traffic. To do this is clearly dangerous and is easily remedied by planning your route good and early. If it is too late to give a signal that other drivers can act upon, you can't turn into that road.

when you signal, you are communicating your intentions, not giving instructions, to other road users. The signal does not give you the right to do anything unless it is safe. You can only know this if you look first.

Avoid confusing others

Direction indicators are the normal way of informing others that you intend to change direction. Make sure that the signal is cancelled after you have completed the manoeuvre.

A right signal means either that you intend to move out to the right, or turn right.

A left signal means you intend to move in to the left, stop on the left or turn left.

– Do not wave pedestrians across the road.

Arm signals

For most occasions when you do intend to change direction, an indicator is better than an arm signal because:

– It can be seen more easily, especially at night

– It can be given for longer

– It allows you to keep both hands on the steering wheel.

But one day your indicators may fail to work, so you should make sure that you know and can give the arm signals shown in the Highway Code.

Never wave pedestrians across the road. You could put them in danger from another vehicle.

Other forms of signal

We have mentioned brake lights in the context of explaining why you need to check your mirrors before braking, remember that early and progressive braking gives drivers behind you time to see your brake lights and warns them that you are slowing down.

The horn is also a signal, but it should only be used to warn of your presence, never used as a rebuke. And never use it when you are close to animals.

Flashing your headlights has the same meaning as sounding your horn. It lets other people know you are there. When another driver flashes his headlights, you must treat this signal as a warning, and

FLA

58

not as an invitation to proceed.

However, if another driver appears to signal in this way to encourage you to go, use your own judgement and proceed carefully. It could be that the headlights weren't flashed at you but at another vehicle waiting to emerge or at a pedestrian about to cross the road. It could also be that the headlights were flashed at you. But it is your decision, and while you should not be hesitant as this could complicate the situation, you must know that it is safe before deciding to go.

Reversing lights are the last thing to mention about giving signals. When you select reverse gear, white lights at the back of most cars indicate to other road users that you are in reverse and probably intend to reverse.

Consider using signals. Don't do things automatically. In each situation choose which signal to use. Think about the necessity and the timing of the signal. And remember that your position and your speed also act as signals informing other road users of your intention to do something. Occasionally they are a far safer alternative to indicating.

Examiner tips

The examiner will expect you to:

– Signal to let others know what you intend doing

– Use your signals to help other road users, including pedestrians

– Always make sure your signal is cancelled after use.

The examiner will also be looking to see that you:

– Give signals clearly and in good time

– Know how to give arm signals and know when they are necessary.

– Treat flashed headlights as a warning, not an invitation to proceed. But if they are flashed as an invitation, it is your decision to accept it, and you must know that it is safe to go.

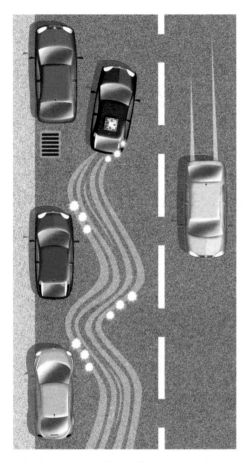

Common problems and reasons for failure

It is a problem when the indicator is going on and off like a yo-yo when going in and out past stationary vehicles (even worse when passing stationary vehicles and not going in and out but still signalling for every car). Failures occur when doing this, if there is a junction on the right and someone thinks you are turning right.

Signal faults tend to be driver faults unless someone is inconvenienced, or unless frequency of missed or wrong signals becomes a pattern of your driving.

Signalling left when asked to turn right: provided you then turn left and not right, is not a failure; the examiner will just take you a different way.

Not knowing arm signals.

– Don't use your indicator like a yo-yo when passing stationary or parked vehicles.

60

Pass Your Driving Test

Section 9

Acting on signs and signals

Knowing your signs and signals for the Theory Test is not enough. Being able to spot them, translate their relevance to you and then act upon them in your everyday driving is of the utmost importance. This is what acting on signs and signals actually means.

Road markings

Everywhere you drive, you will see road signs and markings painted on the road. They are there to help you, and they can only do that if you understand what they all mean. As a general rule, the more paint there is on the road, the more dangers you are likely to encounter.

For example, on a straight stretch of road you will often see painted down the centre short white lines with long gaps between them. As the road nears a bend or junction, the white lines get longer and the gaps are reduced. These are hazard warning lines and advise you of a potential danger ahead. As a safe driver you should be reducing speed and taking extra care when you see these hazard lines.

Traffic-light signals

You must act correctly at traffic-light signals and obey signals given by police officers, traffic wardens and school-crossing patrols. All these signals are given to help you, and to keep the traffic flowing as smoothly as possible. You can cause chaos or danger if you ignore them.

The amber light, for example, can cause problems. The red light follows the amber light. At junctions controlled by traffic lights, there is often very little time delay between your lights going to red and the other traffic's lights going to green. It can be extremely dangerous, if not life-threatening, to come through an amber light. So amber means 'Stop, unless you cannot do so safely.' The 'safely' bit means that if, in stopping, someone will plough into the back of you, it might be too late to stop at the amber light.

– You must obey signals given by police officers, traffic wardens and school-crossing patrols.

But you have to realise that it is possible and important to control the traffic behind you. When you are approaching a hazard, such as traffic lights, you should check behind. If someone is so close that if you have to stop at the lights they would hit you, you should start slowing down immediately, even though the light is still on green. In other words, you should regard amber as meaning 'Stop'. Try thinking 'Stop' on the approach to a green light, rather than 'Go', and you will find that this prepares you for stopping. You shouldn't, of course, do an emergency stop at an amber light.

Signs on your test

On your driving test, the examiner will expect you to follow the road ahead, unless asked to turn, and unless the road signs or markings tell you to do otherwise. Here are some examples of the signs and signals you will meet.

The road ahead is marked with a red sign with a white horizontal bar. This is the No Entry sign. The examiner will not tell you this. You are expected to 'read the road' yourself.

You will almost certainly go through a set of traffic signals. The examiner will expect to see you check that it is safe and clear to drive through, even though the light is showing green.

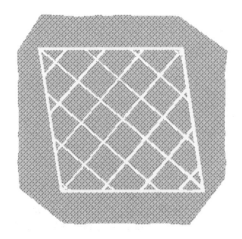

In the middle of a junction you may see a yellow box-grid road marking. You must not enter the yellow box unless your exit is clear. However, you can wait in the box when turning right, as long as it is only the oncoming traffic that prevents you from completing the turn. Your exit must still be clear. Your examiner will expect you to spot road markings like this, and act correctly.

Be aware of the signals that other road users give and act on them sensibly.

If the driver ahead has to wait before turning right, and there is room to overtake on the left, the examiner will expect you to 'read' this situation early and go past on the left.

Sometimes there may be police or traffic wardens controlling the traffic. You will need to know what their signals mean, so that you can comply with them.

Examiner tips

The examiner will expect you to:

– Understand road markings and traffic signs

– React safely and promptly to them.

The examiner will also be looking to see that you:

– Act properly at traffic lights

– Check that the junction is safe before proceeding on a green light.

– Driving through a No Entry sign is a failure.

Common problems and reasons for failure

Going through a Stop sign or through red lights without stopping.

There could be a driver fault for staying out of a bus lane when the time allowed you in.

Passing through the lights at green then seeing the light on the offside far kerb go to red and stopping in the centre of the junction.

Turning right at lights – waiting in the centre for oncoming traffic and either taking too long to move away and finishing up stranded or not knowing that you can go, having passed the stop line. Usually a failure.

Driving through a No Entry sign is a failure.

You get stuck behind a bus signalling left that is obviously pulling up at a bus stop. Do this once and it may be a driver fault. If you follow the bus for a number of stops and pull up each time, then it's a fail.

Section 10

Exercising care in the use of speed

In an earlier section it was explained that one of the biggest difficulties in dealing with junctions is getting the speed right. Once you can control your speed on approach, life becomes much easier, because you have time to look and decide if it is safe to go.

In this section you will take the speed side of things further and learn how to take care in the use of speed in your general driving.

The effects of speed

Modern cars are capable of being driven safely at high speeds, especially on roads designed for this purpose. The average speed of traffic on motorways is, for example, much higher than that of traffic on busy main roads in town. Despite the terrible accidents that occur on motorways, they are, nevertheless, statistically the safest of all our roads. So driving fast is not in itself what causes accidents. But driving too fast in the wrong place at the wrong time can be highly dangerous. The faster you drive, the more you are at risk, so you need to learn how to judge a safe speed for each road on which you are travelling.

The Highway Code advises: 'Drive at a speed that will allow you to stop well within the distance you can see to be clear.'

The less you can see the slower you should drive. It sounds simple but you will find it easier to put into practice if you understand the three main factors that prevent you from seeing well ahead.

– Changing weather conditions can alter visibility dramatically.

1 The road ahead bends round to the right or to the left, or dips suddenly downhill and you cannot see any further.

2 Visibility is poor because it is raining, snowing, foggy, or the sun is low and shining brightly, or it is night time.

3 Traffic or pedestrians make it difficult to see clearly down the road.

In circumstances like these, it does not matter whether or not you are slightly more alert or have faster reactions than another driver. If you are driving too fast, you will have little chance of stopping, however good you are. Commonsense suggests that your only way to stay safe is to slow down. Only time and experience can tell you how much you might need to slow down. Knowing your stopping distances is a fine start, but judging them accurately takes practice.

The diagram on the facing page shows you graphically how to judge your stopping distances when you are approaching a sharp bend in the road.

Trying to imagine the overall stopping distances can help you to understand just how much clear road you need in order to stop safely. You may be amazed at the amount of time it takes you to stop your car, and this may help you slow down to a safe speed.

Try it, it works for most people.

Slowing down to take a sharp bend

Let's imagine you are travelling along at 60mph on a National Speed Limit single carriageway, such as in the diagram below. There is a bend well ahead of you that you cannot see around because of all the trees. If there was a lorry broken down in the bend then you would need to be able to stop safely without hitting it.

– At 60mph it will take 73 metres (240 feet) to stop.

– Imagine you are 73 metres from the bend – you need to start slowing down.

– Now you are 53 metres (175 feet) from the bend. You need to be travelling at 50mph or risk hitting the hidden lorry.

– At 23 metres (75 feet) your maximum speed will need to be 30mph, or you are in deep trouble.

– You reach the bend and can see that, in fact, the road is clear. You can now pick up your speed back to 60mph because the distance you can see to be clear ahead exceeds 73 metres.

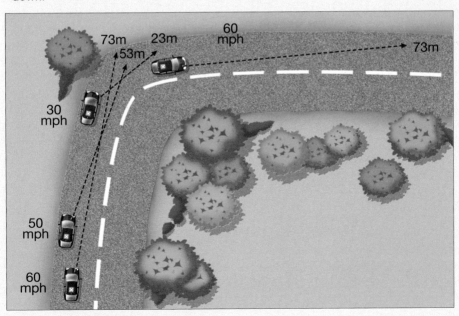

At night, travelling on an unlit road, with your headlights being the only means of giving you a view of the road ahead, you still need to be able to stop within the distance you can see to be clear. This means being able to stop within the range of your headlights.

Poor weather conditions reduce your visibility, but can also reduce your ability to stop quickly.

– When driving around a sharp bend, make sure you can stop safely if a hazard is hidden from your sight as you approach.

Driving in adverse conditions

There will also be times when you are driving in fog and, again, you need to be able to judge your speed so that you can stop well within the distance you can see to be clear. Your speed will depend on your visibility, which in turn will depend on the extent of the fog. If you can see less than 12 metres (40 feet) ahead of you, your speed needs to be less than 20mph. If, however, the fog is more like a light mist, you might be able to see much further and could, therefore, safely drive faster. Heavy rain, snow and a low sun affect your visibility in a similar way, as does driving in the dark.

When the surface of the road is not very good due to rain, or because there is ice, snow, wet leaves or mud on the road, the distance the car will cover before it can come to a standstill is greatly increased.

In wet conditions, you should double your overall stopping distance. You need to be able to see almost twice as far as you could if the road surface was dry, in order to be able to stop within the distance you can see to be clear.

In ice or snow your overall stopping distance can be ten times as much as on a good road surface.

When travelling down a busy high street in the middle of the day with lots of pedestrians and parked cars around, you might not have a lot of space on either side. It is important to remember that people can suddenly step out into the road, car doors can open and vehicles can pull away from the side of the road. You need to judge your speed accordingly and be travelling slowly enough to be able to pull up safely should something dangerous or unpredictable happen.

At 10.30 in the morning, it may be safe to drive along a certain road at 30mph. The same road at 3.30 in the afternoon, when the schools are emptying out, is a very different place. Driving at 30mph then might well be too fast for the conditions.

So slow down whenever your space or vision are restricted and give yourself more time to react according to the conditions.

That covers what you need to know when trying to judge a safe speed for the road, weather and traffic conditions. It may take a long time to learn how to judge a suitable speed, but one of the main things to remember is that you must feel safe. Don't worry about other vehicles behind you making you feel as if you should be driving faster.

– It's hard to judge distances well in foggy conditions.

Examiner tips

The examiner will expect you to:

– Make good progress

– Take account of the road, traffic, weather conditions

– Comply with road signs

– Keep within speed limits.

The examiner will also be looking to see that you:

– Make sure you can stop safely, well within the distance you can see to be clear

– Keep a safe distance on wet or slippery roads.

– Adjust your speed to suit conditions, especially around pedestrians.

Common problems and reasons for failure

Going too fast is not a particularly common reason for failure. While you should not break the speed limits, most examiners like to see someone getting on with it. They will not watch the speedometer like a hawk.

As a rough guide, you will almost certainly fail if you exceed the speed limit by more than around 10mph, or if you constantly drive above the speed limits even if at less than 10mph above them.

If the examiner has to remind you that you are in a speed limit zone, and exceeding the speed limit, you will fail.

Care in the use of speed does not just apply to speed limits. Failure is more likely to happen when you do not take account of the prevailing conditions. For example, going along a road at 20mph when it is crowded with schoolchildren might be construed as not exercising proper care in the use of speed. Failure in such cases is usually the result of a one-off incident rather than a series of errors or totting up.

Erratic changes in your speed can also result in failure.

Section 11

Following behind another vehicle at a safe distance

Having gone through everything to do with controlling your speed and judging a safe speed, this section concludes the subject by explaining separation distances.

Stopping distance

The Highway Code says: 'Leave enough space between you and the vehicle in front so that you can pull up safely if it suddenly slows down or stops.'

At every speed, the safest gap to leave is your overall stopping distance. This is the distance your car will cover before it comes to a standstill, including the time it takes you to react and the time it takes you to brake. It is the minimum distance you would need if you had to use extreme braking to prevent yourself from hitting a brick wall.

When you are following another vehicle and recognise the need to stop quickly, you are, of course, not driving at a brick wall. The car in front of you will cover ground in stopping that you can use

before your car comes to a stop. In an ideal world you would always leave the overall stopping distance between you and the vehicle in front.

In the real world, however, there are huge volumes of traffic to contend with. It might not be practical to leave a gap equivalent to your overall stopping distance. Anyway, it is safe to reduce the gap, but you need to know by how much.

Generally, at speeds over 40mph, if you leave a gap of one metre for every mph of speed, you will be able to stop safely if the vehicle in front of you pulls up suddenly. This distance is extremely difficult to judge. You would find it easier to translate distance into time and use the 'two-second rule'.

– It takes practice to judge a safe gap between you and the vehicle in front.

The two-second rule

A two-second time gap gives you a distance gap of one metre per mph of your speed and it works in the following way:

As the vehicle in front of you passes a stationary object, such as a lamp post or a tree, you count two seconds by saying either 'Only a fool breaks the two-second rule' or by counting 'A thousand and one, a thousand and two.' If you pass the lamp post or tree before you have finished counting, you are too close to the vehicle in front. So you need to

bigger gap than you actually need. You really must never get any closer than your thinking distance – 9 metres at 30mph. At this distance you would probably hit the car in front of you if it stopped suddenly. It is safest to leave your braking distance, and you might find this easiest to judge in car lengths. So, at 30mph a safe gap to leave between you and the vehicle in front would be equivalent to three car lengths.

When it has been raining, or the surface of the road is greasy, you need to increase the gap. Your stopping

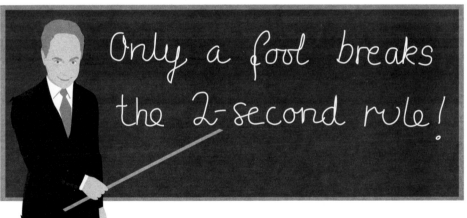

increase the gap and have another go at the next tree or lamp post or whatever.

At speeds of less than 40mph the two-second rule also works perfectly safely, but you are leaving a

distances virtually double, so you would be safest to double the size of the gap.

Another thing to bear in mind is that your view of the road ahead is seriously reduced the closer you get to the vehicle in front. This is especially true if that vehicle happens to be a bus or a lorry. If you hang back you vastly increase what you can see, and therefore improve your chances of reacting early to something that is going to make the bus or lorry driver have to brake suddenly.

As with controlling your speed, judging a safe gap takes time and experience. Go out and practise it, and if someone overtakes you, moving in front, don't feel hassled. Check your mirror and hang back, readjusting the gap to one that is safe between you and the new vehicle in front.

Examiner tips

The examiner will expect you to:

– Drive at a speed so that you can stop within the distance you can see to be clear

– Maintain a safe gap between you and the vehicle in front

– Double the distance in bad conditions.

The examiner will also be looking to see that you:

– Make proper use of the MSM routine

– Show anticipation in your reactions to changing road and traffic conditions and your handling of the controls.

Common problems and reasons for failure

Getting too close to the vehicle in front is a fault which makes an examiner quite jittery. They do not like it. There is nothing worse than being up the exhaust of a bus with virtually no forward vision and having no control of the accelerator. Even a one-off fault under these circumstances may be sufficient to cause a failure.

If the examiner has to tell you to back off you will fail.

If you have to do an Emergency Stop because the vehicle in front stops normally, this would constitute an immediate failure.

Section 12   Making progress

Some drivers have no problem making progress. In fact they drive too fast and become angry with anyone who holds them up. They do not really exercise care in the use of speed. The almost inevitable outcome of this is an accident. Others become over-cautious, too slow and too hesitant. This can create a similar anger in other drivers to that which is experienced by the driver who drives too fast.

You need to be aware that being too hesitant or driving too slowly can be just as dangerous as driving too fast.

Keeping to the speed limit

Our roads are very busy and overcrowded, and the pace of life today makes most people think that they have to be in a hurry. The vast majority of drivers want to arrive at their destination as quickly as is safely possible. Their progress will often be frustrated by the sheer volume of traffic. Most drivers make allowance for this. They expect some traffic jams and hold-ups and set out on their journey with enough time to compensate for the problems. But when they see a clear stretch of road, they want to get moving and make up for lost time.

There is nothing more frustrating than getting stuck for miles behind a driver who appears to be sightseeing – a driver who crawls along at a speed far below the speed limit or below a safe speed for the road conditions. Tempers start to fray and judgement becomes impaired.

You should not exceed the speed limit, but the difference between making progress and not can be the difference between driving to the speed limit of 30mph and travelling along at say 26mph. Driving below the speed limit when it is safe to keep up to the speed limit is unnecessary and frustrating to other drivers.

It is just as irritating as following the sightseer. It can lead to drivers attempting to overtake you where it might not be safe to do so. In turn, this could result in a driver who has overtaken you where the visibility was not good enough – because, for example, there was a brow of a hill ahead – having to cut back in too sharply, clipping the front of your vehicle.

– Road rage can stem from frustration at slower drivers, but it must be avoided at all costs.

– When it's safe to keep up to the speed limit, going slower frustrates other drivers. There's nothing worse than being stuck behind a driver who appears to be sightseeing.

Frustration can easily lead to accidents, and it is little consolation that such an accident was not technically your fault. In recent years there have been a growing number of violent incidents reported on our roads. 'Road rage' is the term usually used to describe such behaviour, and it seems very likely that at least some of the violence has stemmed from the frustration described.

Making progress at junctions

There is another side to the notion of making progress which you need to be aware of, because a similar frustration is often caused. It occurs at junctions and roundabouts. The driver in front of you seems to have fallen asleep, and does not take advantage of gaps in the traffic. While you are an inexperienced driver, you tend to wait for a gap and then get ready to go. By the time you are ready, the gap may have disappeared. When you are more experienced, you will try to anticipate the gap. You will put a lot of energy into looking and continuously asking yourself whether you could go after the next car. If you think this is possible, you will get ready, make your decision and go if it is safe to do so. Because you are ready and have made your decision earlier, you will need a far smaller gap in order to progress safely.

A roundabout is another good example of how undue hesitancy can cause problems. Roundabouts are designed to keep the traffic flowing effectively, and therefore the view on the approach to a roundabout is usually extremely open. You need to match your speed to what you can see. So, on the approach you need to be reducing your speed and looking for a safe gap.

Here is one of the most common accident scenarios. A driver at the front of the queue at a roundabout hesitates and does not take advantage of a safe gap to proceed; the driver behind expects him to go. He sees the gap, assumes that the driver in front has seen it too, expects him to go and moves off before looking back ahead. The result is a nasty dent in the back of one car and a similar dent in the front of the other.

Examiner tips

The examiner will expect you to:

– Make reasonable progress

– Adjust your speed to the road and traffic conditions

– Keep up with traffic

– Emerge at junctions as soon as possible

– Show confidence and judgement.

The examiner will also be looking to see that you select a suitable speed for:

– The type of road

– The volume and type of traffic

– The weather conditions

– Your visibility.

Common problems and reasons for failure

Not making progress is a pet hate of many examiners. This fault is generally a 'build up' one. It seldom happens as a one-incident failure, except in the case of hesitancy at junctions. A one-off here can be when the learner sits and waits when there are frequent safe opportunities to go and finishes up with a great line of frustrated drivers behind.

– Approaching a roundabout, you need to be looking for a safe gap.

Another one-item failure is when slowness makes emerging dangerous. This happens quite often: you look, it is clear, you start to move off and drive out of the junction – but so slowly that before you are anywhere near clear, a vehicle is on top of you. If it is safe, go. Having committed yourself to go, get out of the danger zone as quickly as possible.

It does not take much of this for the examiner to decide that you have no confidence and that a failure is appropriate.

Pass Your Driving Test

Overtaking, meeting and crossing the path of other traffic

Having looked in some detail at how you judge a safe speed – neither travelling too slowly nor too fast for the conditions – this section covers sharing conflicting space. You have already covered in earlier sections some aspects of space management such as, 'space in front when you are following another vehicle', and about 'space on either side', for example on busy streets with parked cars.

The three topics in this section have one thing in common. There is no strict priority and they all involve you potentially coming into conflict with an approaching vehicle if you do not accurately judge how much space you might need.

Overtaking

Overtaking another moving vehicle is potentially the most dangerous driving situation, particularly on single carriageway roads where oncoming traffic will be meeting you head on. A lot of accidents are caused by drivers who overtake in the wrong place or at the wrong time. You really need to practise the skills of overtaking safely before driving alone.

Look for the opportunity to practise the practicalities of overtaking on a dual carriageway. Here you can consider your distance from the vehicle in front, your speed in relation to that vehicle and the use of the MSM routine. Doing this builds your confidence and stands you in

good stead for overtaking a moving vehicle on a two-way road. You can then include in your assessment a consideration of:

a whether it is necessary, safe and legal, and;

b any oncoming traffic as far as space and closing speeds are concerned.

Imagine you are travelling along a National Speed Limit single carriageway and that you are doing the speed limit of 60mph. You see a vehicle ahead of you. You don't know exactly how fast it's going but you know it is travelling slower than you are because you are gaining on it. So let's say it is travelling at 40mph.

– Before overtaking, consider whether the vehicle in front has already indicated it is turning off, making overtaking an unnecessary and risky action.

You now need to ask three questions:

1 Is it necessary to overtake?

2 Is it legal to overtake?

3 Is it safe to overtake?

1 In answering the first question you need to consider:

– Whether the vehicle in front is signalling the intention of turning off the road

– Whether you intend turning off the road shortly yourself

– Whether there is a sign informing you that there is a dual carriageway in half a mile or so

– Whether, as happens in cases other than in the example, the driver is only travelling a couple of mph slower than you are

– Whether you would need to exceed the speed limit in order to overtake.

– When overtaking another vehicle, remember that once you're on the other side of the road your closing speed with an oncoming vehicle is likely to be twice the speed you are doing.

2 It is illegal to overtake where there is a No Overtaking sign or on the approach to a pedestrian crossing, unless it is a moving non-motor vehicle, such as a cyclist.

3 There are places where it is unsafe to overtake, such as:

– Where visibility is poor because there is a bend in the road or where there is a brow of a hill

– Where you can see a junction to the left or to the right and can't be sure that someone isn't waiting to emerge

– Where there is oncoming traffic

– Where the road is not wide enough.

Remember to check your mirrors

because someone may be about to overtake you. Also, think about the speed and the distance away of approaching vehicles. Two vehicles coming towards each other at 55mph will be closing the gap between them at 110mph. That is about 50 metres (165 feet) every second.

Once you have satisfied these three questions, you can proceed with the manoeuvre. You have decided that it is necessary and legal to overtake. It is safe to do so, but not just yet because there are oncoming vehicles. What you now need to do is put into practice a sequence of events called PSLMSM.

Position

You continue gaining on the vehicle in front of you, and at some point you stop gaining on it. That point is where – if you got any closer – you would not be able to see the road ahead. If you were any further back from the vehicle you would not have the power or the time to get past it when a safe opportunity arose. It's like holding your hand in front of your face. The closer you hold your hand to your eyes, the less you can see of what is happening in front of it, but the further away you hold your hand, the more you can see.

Speed

In maintaining this position from the vehicle in front you must now have slowed to the same speed. So you have matched your speed to that of the other vehicle, 40mph, and in doing so you may

need to change down a gear from fifth to fourth or even third to give you sufficient power to overtake when the road ahead is clear.

Look

You are now checking the road ahead to see whether it is still necessary, legal and safe to overtake and, in particular, you are looking for a safe gap.

Mirrors

Imagine that the road ahead is now clear and you can start your manoeuvre. Check behind to see if it is safe to move out.

Signal

Usually a signal is necessary if only to inform the driver in front that you intend overtaking. The driver might be masking a cyclist or smaller vehicle that they themselves intend overtaking, and your signal could prompt them to warn you of their intentions.

Manoeuvre

Move out smoothly and swiftly, leaving plenty of room between you and the other vehicle and making sure that you can see the vehicle in your interior mirror before you move back in to the left. It is not usually necessary to signal your intentions to move back in because that is what you are expected to do anyway.

On your driving test you may well catch up with slow-moving traffic. The examiner will expect you to overtake any slow-moving traffic when it is safe to do so.

If you are in a situation where you need to overtake a cyclist, the problem is deciding just how much room they should have. It is wise to imagine that they are a lot wider than they are and to aim to leave them the same amount of space as you would for a parked car. They may wobble or swerve suddenly.

Remember to check behind before deciding to overtake any cyclist.

– Imagine cyclists are a lot wider than they are and give them a wide berth.

If someone is overtaking you, or it would cause problems with oncoming traffic, it is not safe. So, if you cannot go straight past, you will need to slow down in order to follow at a safe distance.

Don't ever feel pressured into overtaking. If you are in any doubt at all about the safety of it, don't do it.

Meeting

Where the road is narrowed to less than the width of two vehicles and there is a vehicle approaching you from the opposite direction, you are coming into a meeting situation.

It is a hazard because you will be both using the same space, so you need to start the hazard routine of MSM. Check behind to see the position and speed of any following vehicles. The signal you need to consider first is your brake lights.

While you are slowing down, you need to assess the actions of the approaching driver in order to come through the gap separately. In slowing down early you are giving yourself plenty of time to decide what to do next.

Sometimes the approaching driver will come through the gap before you and you can then safely use the MSM routine to accelerate again. Sometimes the approaching driver will also be slowing down, resulting in both of you reaching the gap at the same time. In this instance, you will need to be looking for a safe place to stop to allow the other driver to come through the gap first.

– Meeting in a narrow street is a hazard because you will both be sharing the available space.

The road can be narrowed by a number of things:

1 You might be travelling along a road with parked cars on either side, in which case you need to be looking for gaps into which you could pull or opposite which you could wait, should an approaching vehicle come along. If you pull into a gap, remember to leave yourself plenty of room to pull away again and to check behind to consider a signal before doing so.

2 There may be roadworks ahead, narrowing the road to less than the width of two vehicles. As before, try to time your approach speed so that you can keep the car moving through the gap created by the obstruction.

3 You might be travelling along a narrow country lane, in which case keep an eye open for passing places into which you can pull or opposite which you can wait should an approaching vehicle come along.

There is a priority stated in the Highway Code that says where the obstruction is on your side of the road you should give way to any approaching traffic. Where, however, the obstruction is on the opposite side of the road you should not assume that an oncoming vehicle will give way to you. Use the MSM routine and slow down to give you more time to assess the situation.

Sometimes from a distance it is difficult to assess the size of the gap. As you get closer, you may decide that it's big enough for both vehicles to pass safely. You will still need to slow down in the first place in order to make an accurate assessment. Also, in order to leave adequate clearance on both sides, you will need a reduced speed. Where there is less space, less speed will increase your reaction time should something go wrong.

Meeting traffic safely depends on your use of the MSM routine. Anywhere that you spot a narrowing of the road ahead, for whatever reason, check your mirrors and slow down. If you are tempted to force your way through by holding your ground, think. What if the other driver hasn't seen you? What if the other driver assumed there was enough space for both of you, when there clearly isn't?

Crossing

Finally in this section, you need to think about crossing the path of other vehicles. This is also a situation where you could be coming into conflict with another vehicle because you both have to use the same space or piece of road.

When you turn right from a major into a minor road you usually have to cross the path of oncoming traffic. You must learn to judge how much time you need in order to make your turn safely. If you are able to anticipate a gap in the traffic, you may be able to slow down and complete your turn without ever having to stop.

If your car is still moving, you can make safe use of smaller gaps in the oncoming traffic. But once your car has stopped, you need extra time to get it moving again. Oncoming vehicles should not

– If you pull into a gap to let someone by, leave enough space to get out.

have to stop, slow down or swerve to allow you to complete the turn.

If the road is busy, you will often have to stop and wait for a safe gap.

If this is the case, make sure you position your car correctly. This position is normally just to the left of the centre of the road. Look for gaps in the oncoming traffic.

In judging a safe gap, look at the approaching traffic and ask yourself whether you would walk across the road in front of that car. If the answer is 'yes', make your turn. If the answer is 'no' or 'I don't know', don't go.

Examiner tips

The examiner will expect the following from you:

1 Overtaking
  – Allow enough room, especially for cyclists, motorcyclists and horse riders

  – Allow enough room after overtaking and avoid cutting in.

2 Meeting
  – Meet and deal with traffic safely and confidently

  – Use the MSM routine

  – Slow down and be prepared to stop

– You must learn to judge how much time you need in order to make your turn safely.

– Keep well back from an obstruction if you need to stop, so you can see ahead and will have the room to move off again.

3 Crossing

– Use the MSM routine

– Position correctly and adjust your speed

– Watch out for oncoming traffic and stop if necessary

– Watch out for pedestrians crossing at the side road.

The examiner will also be looking at the following:

1 Overtaking

– Consider the speed and position of any vehicles behind or coming towards you

– Overtake only when it is safe and you will not cause other vehicles to slow down or alter course.

2 Meeting

– Show judgement in meeting situations

– Be decisive when stopping or moving off.

3 Crossing

– Show sound judgement before turning across the path of approaching traffic.

Common problems and reasons for failure

Usually an overtaking fault is always a serious fault and would lead to failure.

Overtaking

Having to be stopped by the examiner before actually starting, or getting back in by the skin of your teeth because of poor judgement is a common fault.

Another common fault is pulling in too quickly. Remember to check your mirrors after overtaking before pulling back in.

Meeting

Faults usually occur by failing to observe developing situations sufficiently far ahead.

A common misconception is that if the obstruction is on the offside, then you have the right of way. If someone is committed to coming through, you should give way irrespective of which side the obstruction is on. Many pupils ask examiners what they should do if facing another car nose to nose when they have failed to anticipate the obvious. If you get into this position you should immediately try to rectify it rather than ask what to do.

Crossing

This is a problem when turning right and not appreciating the speed of oncoming vehicles. This is a very hairy situation for examiners because it often happens out of the blue and you are broadside on across the bows of a speeding vehicle. The impact is going to be on the examiner's side. It only takes six feet of forward movement of the learner car to be in this position.

Another problem is not appreciating that if you have moved the first six feet, it is best to go and go quickly. Quite often a perfectly safe crossing can become dangerous because of the slow speed at which it is done. This fault often happens at traffic lights. You see the lights in front of you turn to amber and set off. You pay no attention to oncoming traffic which is travelling at speed and has no chance of stopping at the line.

– Don't ask your examiner to get you out of an unanticipated meeting situation.

Section 14   Reversing around a corner

Some new drivers have heard stories that say everyone finds reversing difficult and, because they believe them, they go on to find reversing their car hard and mess it up.

In reality, reversing a car is no more difficult than going forwards, but going backwards can make steering feel different because the front wheels, which make the car turn, are now at the 'wrong end' of the car.

The need for reversing

When you have passed your test, you will need to reverse frequently in everyday driving. You may, for example, have driven up the wrong road. If the road is not wide enough to turn around, you will need to reverse around a corner to the left or right.

It is advisable to learn how to reverse both to the left and to the right because you will find this increases your options. For example, when you drive to the supermarket and need to park your car, you can choose whether to reverse into a space on either the left or the right. If there is a driveway leading to your house, you should reverse into it. This means that you can then drive forwards onto the road, which is far safer than reversing because you have much better visibility. By being able to carry out both the left and the right reverses it would not matter from which direction you approached your house.

Reversing can be dangerous, because other drivers and pedestrians do not necessarily expect you to be doing it. A pedestrian may step into the road behind your car because, even if they see you at the wheel, they will be expecting you to move off forwards. So you must take care and keep looking. You must not cause inconvenience or danger to other drivers or pedestrians.

– If there is a driveway leading to your house, you should reverse into it.

Your vision to the rear is more restricted than when looking forwards, so it is important that you do not just rely on the view of your mirrors to tell you what is happening behind. Ensure that you look over your shoulder through the rear window and that you are prepared to give way to anything that might be in your path.

Comfort when reversing

When you are reversing in a straight line or round to the left, it can be uncomfortable and awkward to look over your left shoulder for any length of time, so it's advisable to alter your position in the seat. Turn in the seat so that your body and not just your head is to the left. In this position you need to check that you can still reach the pedals easily, and you may need to move the seat closer.

You may now find it easier to hold the wheel with your right hand at the top and your left hand at the bottom. If you find this awkward, you may also rest your left

– Remember that you can surprise other drivers and pedestrians because they don't necessarily expect you to be reversing.

hand on the back of the passenger seat or on the edge of your seat and reverse with just one hand on the wheel. The most important things are that you have the best view to the rear of the car through the rear windscreen and that you can maintain this view throughout the manoeuvre, while maintaining full control of the car.

– You may support your backward-looking position by resting your left hand on the back of the passenger seat.

– Watch for pedestrians and oncoming vehicles as the front of the car swings out when reversing around a corner.

good look all around, including into blindspots, and that you are prepared to give way to anyone who might be there.

Looking backwards can seem strange and may cause you to turn the steering wheel in the wrong direction. It's a good idea to practise reversing in a straight line before you attempt to reverse around a corner. You will find that only tiny movements of the steering wheel are necessary in order to keep the car straight. Try to focus on an object a long way down the road behind the car. This will help you to judge whether you are travelling in a straight line.

Reversing during the test

On your driving test, if you are asked to do a reverse around a corner, it could be to the left or right. If you are driving a van with poor visibility to the rear and sides, you will be asked to demonstrate a reverse to the right. You can be far safer, and see more by looking out of the driver's door window, than you could if you were reversing to the left and trying to see out of the passenger's door window.

When driving forwards you need to update yourself constantly on what is happening behind by glancing in the rearview mirror, because what is happening behind will affect the decisions you need to make. In a similar way, while reversing you need to update yourself on what is happening ahead. During a reversing manoeuvre you are looking in the direction of travel but you also need to make frequent checks forward to see what the situation is and whether there is any need to give way to other road users, including pedestrians.

When reversing around a corner, the front end of the car will swing out into the middle of the road. It is, therefore, extremely important that just before you intend turning the wheel, you have a

On your test, the examiner will ask you to stop by the side of the road just before a side road or opening. He will ask you to drive past the junction, then reverse into it, and to keep reversing back for a reasonable distance. This, in practice, means about three to four car lengths when reversing to the left, more if reversing to the right. You should:

– Drive past the turning

– Look into the turning for any problems as you drive past

– Stop in a position from which you can reverse safely into it.

Stop about 40 centimetres away from the kerb and at least two-plus car lengths beyond the corner. Make sure you are parallel to the kerb and that you stop with your wheels straight. Remember to turn slightly in your seat, so that you can see to the rear through the back window.

– As you pass the turning you are reversing into, check the side road to see if there are any problems.

Never reverse simply by looking in your mirrors. Look all around before you start to reverse. When you reverse, you must keep the car under full control, keep reasonably close to the kerb and look out for other traffic and pedestrians. Look out particularly for children, who may be hidden behind the car (if necessary, get out and look).

Remember as you turn the wheel that the front end of your car will swing out into the road, so look forwards and all around just before you turn the wheel. Keep looking all around the whole of the time you are moving backwards. Use clutch control to reverse at a safe speed.

You may remove your seatbelt when reversing, but remember to put it back on again before you drive off.

You need to keep the car moving at a walking pace in order to reverse it where you want it to be. At the same time you can keep looking around you to make sure it is all safe. You achieve this walking pace with clutch control or brake control.

Remember that clutch control is the ability to move the car at a very slow speed and stop it again by using a constant gas pressure and fractional clutch movements. It should be used in reverse or first gear.

If you are reversing downhill, clutch control is ineffective, because in raising

93

the clutch you are simply driving the car in the same direction as gravity is pulling it. So you need brake control. Brake control allows you to keep the car moving at a very slow speed by holding the clutch just below the biting point and feathering the foot brake.

Now you know where you should look, what you should look for and how to sit so that you can most easily see. You also know how to steer and how your car will react when you steer.

Having got through all that, now you need to learn how to actually reverse around a left-hand corner.

The Left Reverse

Drive slowly past the junction on the left, checking to see that it is safe, legal and convenient to carry out the manoeuvre.

The task is split into three parts so that it is easier to see what you have to do:

1 You reverse in a straight line

2 You steer around the corner

3 You reverse in a straight line again.

1 The first thing you do is reverse to the 'point of turn', when you will need to steer. Start the manoeuvre so that you are clear of the junction and not restricting anyone's visibility should they wish to emerge – about two to three car lengths is safe. Position the car parallel to the kerb and roughly 40 centimetres away, with the wheels straight. This will give you room to correct any slight errors without risk of touching the kerb. Try looking well down the road and noting where the kerb cuts into the rear windscreen. If you keep the kerb in relation to the rear windscreen in the same place, then the car will remain on a straight course. The point of turn is where the rear wheel nearest the kerb lines up with the start of the corner – the first curved kerbstone. The problem is that through the metal bodywork of the car you cannot see the rear wheel from the driver's seat. Therefore, you need to identify something you can see that indicates you are at the point of turn. Some people do this on judgement and can accurately assess where the rear wheel is in relation to the kerb, others practise through trial and error, and others use a method.

2 You now need to judge how much you should turn the wheel in order to get the car around the corner. If you are at a sharp corner you will usually find that you'll need full left lock. You need to steer quickly and fully to the left while keeping the car moving very slowly, and don't forget to have a good look all around before you start to steer.

Try to notice the new road, or the straight kerbstones, coming into the rear windscreen. When the straight kerbstones cut into the rear windscreen at almost the same point they did at the start of the manoeuvre, that tells you the car is almost parallel to the kerb and it is time to straighten the wheels.

3 The last part of the manoeuvre is a straight reverse. Reverse clear of the junction by about three car lengths.

– Making a successful reverse around a corner is an art which some practise through trial and error; others find themselves a method...

If the corner around which you are about to reverse is a gentle sweeping curve, you won't need to steer so hard. You will normally be able to keep sight of the corner throughout the manoeuvre.

Often you are at the point of turn when the kerbstones are about to disappear behind the car's rear pillar. It is difficult to give a precise point on which to focus because of the various shapes and sizes of cars and also because each driver is closer or further away from the wheel depending on their height and build.

Once you have established where you need to be focusing, you simply keep the kerb in exactly the same place by turning the wheel slowly and steadily to the left and back again as necessary.

When you can see only straight kerbstones in the rear windscreen, the corner is passed and you need to allow the back end of the car to move in towards the kerb. Do this until you can see the kerbstones again cutting in through the rear windscreen almost where they were at the start. That is the time to straighten the wheels.

Remember that you are the obstruction; and if another vehicle wishes to emerge from the junction into which you are reversing, then you are in the way and you need to be prepared to pull forwards and start the manoeuvre again once the other driver has gone.

The Right Reverse

There are important differences between the right and the left reverse. These differences are to do with your observations.

1   With the right reverse, you are reversing with the flow of traffic. This means that you need to make frequent forward checks and be prepared to give way to any traffic on your side of the road.

2   As you reverse around the corner and are about to disappear from the view of any vehicles on the major road, you need to pause and look. If a vehicle wishes to enter the road into which you are reversing, they will of course be driving directly into your path. Make sure that they have seen you. Then continue reversing a short way so that the driver can turn safely without cutting the corner.

3   Once you are in the new road and have straightened up the wheels, you need to reverse approximately twice as far as you did on the left reverse. This gives you plenty of room to move away and position yourself on the left-hand side of the road again, ready to emerge. Remember that because you are moving away from the right-hand side of the road, you need to check your left blindspot this time.

– Make sure any vehicle wanting to turn into the road you are reversing into has seen you.

To start the manoeuvre, pull up on the left-hand side of the road just before the junction on the right around which you are going to reverse. As you move away, take up a position in the road as close to the left of the centre as is safe, as though you were going to do a right turn, but do not give a right-hand signal at this stage. As you pass the junction on the right, have a look into it to see whether it is safe, legal and convenient to carry out the manoeuvre. Give a right-hand signal if necessary and, once the road is clear, move over to the right-hand side of the road and stop the car about three car lengths from the junction, parallel to and about 40 centimetres from the kerb.

You now reverse in a straight line until you get to the point of turn. Keep the car moving slowly and observe over your left shoulder, because this will give you the best view of the road behind. As the corner disappears from view through the rear windscreen, switch to your right shoulder. This means you can now see the kerb and judge how little or how much you need to turn the wheel in order to steer the car around the corner.

Remember to keep checking forwards and also to have a good look all around the vehicle before you begin to steer. Start to steer as soon as you can see that the rear offside wheel is at the start of the corner. As the car comes round the corner, straighten the wheels and again observe through the rear windscreen over your left shoulder. This allows you to see well down the road behind you. An occasional glance over your right shoulder, to check the position of the car in relation to the kerb, is acceptable.

Remember to pause to see and be seen before you disappear into the junction, and then continue reversing slowly in a straight line until you are well clear of the junction, about six car lengths. If there are hazard road markings, you could reverse until you were clear of those.

Examiner tips

The examiner will expect you to reverse:

– Smoothly

– Correctly

– Safely

– Under control

– Keeping reasonably close to the kerb

– Without mounting or hitting the kerb

– Without swinging out too wide.

The examiner will also be looking to see that you:

– Check traffic and road conditions

– Look out for traffic and pedestrians

– Stop in a safe position.

Common problems and reasons for failure

You need to ensure that the vehicle does not run away and that you are reasonably accurate.

Accuracy means a reasonable line around the corner, not a great loop or over the kerb. About a foot away would be fine provided that the line is right.

Candidates often fail to use the brake if there is a slight hill downwards.

If the wheel touches the kerb, don't panic. Use your head. Pull forward sufficiently to straighten up and then go backwards again.

Do not wait for the examiner to tell you what to do. Doing it on your own shows that you are aware of where your car is in relation to the kerb.

As you steer, the front of the car swings out. Look before you steer, not afterwards, by which time it would be too late.

If traffic approaches from the side road, hold back. See what is happening and if necessary pull forward around the corner. Let the traffic clear and start again. Don't wait to be asked by the examiner. Show you can make decisions.

– After the manoeuvre, the examiner will expect you to stop the car in a safe position.

Section 15   Turning in the road

Unless you decide to drive a London taxi, which can turn around in a remarkably small circle, you are certain to need to make use of this skill; that is, how to turn your car to face in the opposite direction using forward and reverse gears.

Not a three-point turn

If there are no side roads or openings you can reverse into, and the road is not wide enough to allow you to make a U-turn, you will need to turn your car around by a series of forward and backward movements. This is often, but incorrectly, called a three-point turn. The number of movements needed to complete the turn will depend on the width of the road, the length of your car, its steering lock and your ability to handle the controls.

The skills involved are also very useful for getting yourself out of a tight parking position. You may need to move the car forwards and backwards, steering to full lock and back again several times before you can move away.

On your driving test, the examiner will ask you to pull up on the left at a convenient place. He will expect you to complete the exercise in as few moves as possible, without touching the kerb. You must show you are in full control of the car, keep looking all around and be careful not to cause any danger to other traffic or pedestrians.

Make sure you have stopped in a suitable place. Move along the road a little if necessary before you start. It is silly to find, for example, that you are driving or reversing straight towards a lamp post on the edge of the kerb. So don't make life difficult. Allow yourself a little margin for error. You may remove your seatbelt to complete the manoeuvre.

The minimum number of moves you can make for a Turn in the Road is three, so

– To make the Turn in the Road, stop in a suitable place, with plenty of room to manoeuvre.

let's look at how you would put this into practice, referring to the diagram on page 102.

The first of the three moves involves taking the car from a parked position on the left-hand side of the road and steering it across the road, ideally aiming for a 90° angle to the kerb. You must wait to steer until the car is moving and then get full right lock on in the shortest possible distance. Keep that lock on for as long as you dare, leaving yourself enough time and room to steer the wheels back to the left without hitting the kerb.

You need to steer the wheels back to the left because when you start reversing in the second part of the manoeuvre, the back end of the car needs to move to the left first. If you stop with the wheels still on full right lock, when you start reversing the car will move in the direction from which it has just come and you risk not completing the manoeuvre. It is only necessary to straighten the wheels or get them turned just slightly to the left.

Have a good look all around the car before you start moving and do not move if you see a vehicle coming towards you from either direction; let them go first.

Once you're a driver it is easy to overlook pedestrians, but you must look out for them anyway. They can easily be alarmed if they see you turning your car across the road towards them.

– Don't alarm pedestrians when you are turning across the road towards them.

Once you start the manoeuvre, look mainly right as you steer right and left as you steer left. This keeps you focusing in the direction from which your immediate danger is coming.

You should avoid hitting the kerb, although if you just touch it through a lack of judgement then you will not fail your test. If you bounce up the kerb through a lack of control, you could endanger pedestrians and this would be marked as a serious fault.

You therefore need to keep the car moving reasonably slowly, using clutch control. Take care as the car comes over the crown of the road as, depending on the severity of the camber, you may need to switch to brake control to prevent the car rolling away from you.

When you complete the first part of the manoeuvre you will usually need to put

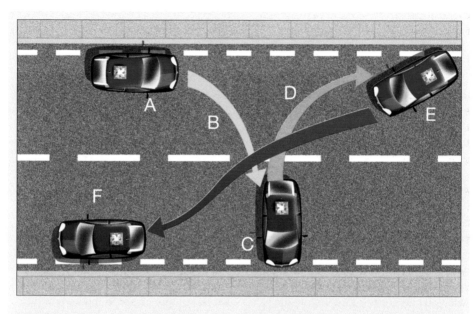

Use clutch control to creep slowly forwards (A), turning the wheel quickly and fully to the right. Keep looking all around (B).

When the front of the car is about a metre from the kerb, steer quickly to the left, braking to a stop before the front wheels touch the kerb (C). Look at the camber of the road. The curve in the road surface may cause the car to speed up.

Put on the hand brake, and prepare to reverse. Use clutch control to hold the car still, and look all around before moving backwards.

Use clutch control to creep slowly

backwards (D), steering quickly to the left. Keep looking all around, particularly over your right shoulder. The right side of the car will reach the kerb first.

When the back of the car is about a metre from the kerb, steer quickly to the right. Brake to a stop just before the boot of the car overhangs the kerb, and before the rear wheels touch the kerb (E).

Put on the hand brake and prepare to move the car forwards. Look all around before moving. Drive slowly forwards, steering as necessary to reach the left-hand side of the road (F). Park on the left, and put your seatbelt back on.

on the hand brake so that the car doesn't roll into the kerb.

For the second part, you need to select reverse gear and get the car ready for an uphill start. Have a good look all around, especially over both shoulders through the rear windscreen and at the pavement towards which you will be reversing. Give way to any pedestrians.

As you start to move, steer quickly and fully to the left. Keep observing over your left shoulder through the rear windscreen and, as you cross the crown of the road, switch your observations to over your right shoulder. Your immediate danger would now be coming from the right. Also you can better judge the proximity of the kerb as the offside rear wheel is closest to it. About a metre from the kerb start steering to the right and stop the car just before you get to the kerb. Again, when taking the lock off, it is only necessary to straighten the wheels or get

them turned just slightly to the right so that when you move away the car will head off to the right.

Now comes the third part of the manoeuvre. You will need to put on the hand brake, select first gear and, if there is a camber, prepare for an uphill start. Have a good look all around and give way to any other road users. When it is safe, move off slowly, steering to the right.

It is at this point that you can decide whether in fact you can complete the manoeuvre in three turns or whether you need five. If you think you are going to mount the kerb, steer the wheels to the left as you get closer to the kerb and stop. You will need to repeat parts two and three of the manoeuvre.

Problems can arise when another vehicle appears on the scene while you are in the middle of carrying out this

– If you're in the middle of the manoeuvre and another car turns up, look to see if the driver intends letting you complete the turn.

and let you complete the manoeuvre. Let them make the decision rather than you beckoning them through, as you may be putting them at unnecessary risk if you haven't noticed something coming from the other direction. If the other driver is obviously going to wait for you, don't hang about, but also don't panic. There is a temptation to rush because someone is waiting – don't give in to it. Rushing easily causes mistakes, so be warned.

Start by practising on very quiet roads and progress to roads where other traffic is likely to appear. In that way you get used to coping with the pressure of the situation. It is a good idea to try out this exercise when facing both up and down fairly steep hills so that you get used to the different moments when you will need clutch or brake control.

– Practise making turns in the road on fairly steep hills to get the feel for both brake and clutch control.

manoeuvre. Usually, it is best to complete the part of the turn you are doing. The other driver has far more chance of being able to steer around you than if you had stopped in the middle of the road. Your best bet is to look at the other driver to see what they intend doing.

Allow them to make up their own minds about whether they wish to drive past you or whether they are going to wait

– Don't frustrate your examiner by being so slow that you hold up the whole town.

Examiner tips

The examiner will expect you to turn your car around in the road:

– Smoothly

– Under control

– Making proper use of the accelerator, clutch, brakes and steering

– Without touching or mounting the kerb.

The examiner will also be looking to see that you:

– Are aware of other road users

– Keep looking all around throughout the manoeuvre.

Common problems and reasons for failure

Many learners find it difficult to turn the steering wheel quickly while they are trying to keep the car moving slowly.

This manoeuvre often goes wrong in the first two seconds. If you allow the car to lurch forwards, you are halfway across the road before much steering is done, and then things go from bad to worse.

On the reverse leg learners often look towards the offside rear wheel to see how close to the kerb they are. Because of a lack of steering in the first place, the nearest wheel is in fact the rear nearside, and thus they mount the kerb.

A regular problem is being unable to control your car on a steep camber and forgetting to switch from clutch control

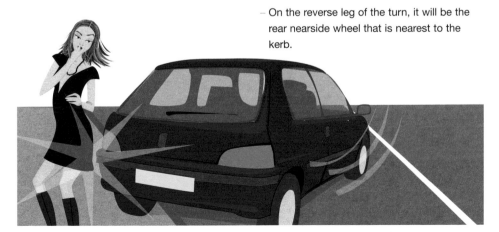

– On the reverse leg of the turn, it will be the rear nearside wheel that is nearest to the kerb.

to brakes when the car starts to run forward.

Observations often take place far too early, before the car is ready to move. By the time you do move, a car is there, which had not been there when you looked. The observation should be done immediately before moving. Look more than once if necessary.

Often people take so long to do the exercise that observation is required again halfway across the road. For example, a pedestrian has appeared and is not seen.

Many people believe they must do the exercise in three moves, and just as many think that it doesn't matter how many it takes. The examiner expects it to be done in a reasonable number of turns, depending on the width of the road and size of the car.

Examiners get very frustrated by anyone who controls the car and looks carefully, but does the whole thing an inch at a time and so slowly that the whole town is brought to a standstill. The examiner might have a job justifying a fail in these circumstances, but show hesitancy in your normal driving and you would likely fail for lack of progress.

A word of warning
Learner drivers are advised not to practise on test routes, particularly as this might cause upset to local residents. Be very careful where you practise this exercise – or reversing around corners – and how often you do it in the same place.

Section 16

Reverse parking

Next time you're feeling in need of a little light entertainment, take a stroll down a busy high street where roadside parking is allowed for limited periods of time. Watch drivers attempting to park by reversing into a gap between two parked cars. You will see an extraordinary variety show, from superb, controlled skill to complete farce, from perfection to dismal failure.

This is no different to anywhere else on the road, you may say, but in this instance the reason may partly lie with the fact that most of the driving population has never been taught how to reverse park safely or accurately.

Parking in a car park

You will seldom find a safe and suitable parking space easy to come across, especially in town. But the ability to reverse into a parking space will help you enormously because it allows you to make use of smaller gaps.

In fact, in today's traffic conditions it has become essential that you can perform this task safely and efficiently, and without holding up other traffic for longer than absolutely necessary.

Whenever you can, it is safest and easiest to park in a car park. Most car parks are marked out in bays, which clearly show you where you are allowed to park.

Because many car parks operate a one-way system, you are also likely to see arrows and signs showing you where

– Before reverse parking, make sure the chosen space is actually big enough.

to go. Not only are car parks very busy places, but the spaces inside them are often quite small. When you have found an empty bay, it is usually simplest and safest to reverse into it. Your car is more manoeuvrable in reverse gear, which makes it easier to fit into the available gap. Look all around your car for any dangers before moving backwards. When you are ready to leave, you can drive out forwards. This makes it much easier to see other vehicles and pedestrians.

Reverse parking between two vehicles

Imagine that you are driving through a busy high street shopping area. You need to park your car and there is a stream of parked cars already lining the road. There is also a lot of moving traffic behind and ahead of you. You are travelling slowly, looking for a space, and you think you can see one. You now check behind to see how close the following traffic is. You indicate to the left and you gently brake so as to pull up just before the gap. This now gives you the chance to assess the suitability of the gap. You need to decide whether it is:

1   Safe. Is it on a bend or near the brow of a hill or too close to a junction? Is there broken glass in the gutter? Are there pedestrians using the gap to cross the road? Are there children playing?

2   Convenient. Is there a driveway in the gap, or might somebody need access

– Check whether there are any parking restrictions because other drivers might take a risk in parking where they shouldn't.

to the entrance or to a garage? Are you going to narrow the road too much by carrying out a reverse park?

3 Legal. Do parking restrictions prevent you from parking there at all, or are you limited to a certain amount of time?

4 Suitable. You should consider any gradient and the necessary techniques to control the speed. You also need to consider the camber, because if it is steep the car will have a tendency to roll away as soon as you steer to the right to bring the front end into the gap, unless you use brake control.

The other thing to consider is that you need a minimum space of one and a half times the length of your own vehicle in order to be able to manoeuvre your car into the gap. Probably a space of at least twice the length of your vehicle would be best.

Now, fairly obviously, you cannot take all day to make up your mind or you'll cause miles of traffic jams behind you. So you must think quickly and with confidence.

If, after considering all these things, you decide that your choice of site is suitable, check your mirrors and slowly pull forwards. Often people are not sure of your intentions. If you pull up immediately in front of the gap, ready to reverse into it, you may find that the following vehicle has pulled up right behind you, preventing you from reversing into your selected space. If you pull up before the gap you have a better chance of assessing it and of allowing other road users to understand your intentions.

You may need to indicate to the left again as you stop ahead of the gap. Also, remember that your brake lights act as a signal and inform other road users that you are not moving off. Select reverse

109

– Make your intention to park clear, or you may find the following vehicle has pulled too close behind you and blocked your access.

gear as soon as you can. This is a useful signal and, in selecting reverse, you can cancel your indicator. Now you are ready to reverse into the gap.

The speed of your car matched to the speed at which you turn the wheel, where and when you look, and your accuracy, are all crucial to how successful you are in parking your car first time. So don't dawdle, but do take your time and, within reason, don't worry about holding up the other traffic.

It is better to take it steady and get into the space in one go, than to feel harassed, rush things, find that you hit

the kerb and have to reposition to start the whole thing again.

Take great care with where and when you look. Bear in mind that pedestrians often cross the road in gaps; children can break free from adults and run into the road; dogs can also run out especially if they are chasing a cat. Vehicles coming up behind you may choose to steer around you, and in doing so may need to move into the path of oncoming traffic, so be prepared to give way.

Make sure you look out for all these things, especially before you start to steer, because the front end of the car will swing out, narrowing the width of the road even more. Remember to look mainly over your left shoulder through the rear windscreen, which is the direction in which the car is moving.

It is recommended that until you have reasonable experience you only practise this exercise with an Approved Driving Instructor and in a car with dual controls.

For your first few attempts, you should select a very quiet road where you will cause least inconvenience to other traffic. It is important that you warn any other drivers of your intention by giving an early signal when necessary.

When practising, take care not to annoy local residents.

Also, remember that car owners can become very nervous if they see you getting too close to the vehicle which is their pride and joy. So to start with, choose a gap of at least two to three car lengths in order to allow a safety margin for error. As your skills improve, you can gradually select smaller gaps.

One method of reverse parking

Some people do a reverse parking manoeuvre through judgement, others through trial and error, others by comparing it to their experience of the other manoeuvres, in particular the left reverse, and others do it by using a method.

There are plenty of methods from which you can choose. They are all variations on the same theme.

– Pedestrians use gaps in parked cars to cross the road – remember that before parking.

111

No one method suits everyone, and your best bet is to let your driving instructor help you decide which one is likely to help you the most. But do remember that a method is simply a means of practising the manoeuvre successfully until you are good enough at it to be able to use your own judgement. Then you can adapt the speed, steering, accuracy and your observations to suit the particular situation in which you find yourself.

One commonly used method is shown below. It works in a Vauxhall Corsa or other cars of a similar size.

When you pull up alongside the front parked car, aim to stop just forwards of it, about one metre away, and making sure that you are parallel to it and that your wheels are straight. Check all around, and reverse very slowly. As soon as the backs of the two cars are level with each other, turn the wheel one and a half times to the left. Try matching your steering to the speed of the car and avoid turning the wheel when the car is stationary. Remember to have another look around before you start to steer.

Look over your left shoulder, and as you see the door mirror of your car line up with the end of the other car, turn the steering wheel one and a half times to the right. This will, of course, straighten the wheels of the car and allow you to reverse at the angle you have just created.

Continue reversing, looking backwards and glancing forwards, until you see the offside corner of the other vehicle through the tax disc or in the bottom left-hand corner of your front windscreen. Steer one

1. Gap should be 1½ car lengths.

2. Stop parallel to front parked car, about one metre away.

3. Reverse until the backs of the cars are level and turn the wheel 1½ times to the left. Remember that the car front will swing out as you move.

4. As you see the door mirror of your car line up with the back of the other car, turn the steering wheel 1½ times to the right.

5. When you see the offside corner of the other car in the bottom-left corner of your windscreen, steer 1½ times to the right.

6. When you are almost parallel with the kerb steer 1½ times to the left to straighten the wheels and stop.

7. If necessary, move backwards or forwards to straighten up.

– It's important to remember that in the test there may not actually be a car defining the rear of the space, in which case use your imagination.

and a half times to the right. This will bring the front end of the car in towards the kerb.

When you are almost parallel with the kerb, steer one and a half times to the left to straighten the wheels and stop. If necessary, move backwards or forwards to straighten up.

Reverse parking in the test
The reverse parking exercise you may be required to carry out on the driving test could either be on the road or in an off street parking area at the driving test centre. So let us deal with these separately.

On road reverse park
You will first be asked to park the car, on the left, just behind another parked car, leaving yourself enough room to move away again. The examiner will then ask you to pull out forwards, around the other car and stop alongside it, before reversing towards the kerb to finish

parallel and close to it, and completing the manoeuvre within two car lengths. It is important to understand that on many occasions there will not be a car actually parked to define the rear of the space into which you are going to reverse.

You should signal if necessary, drive alongside the car pointed out by the examiner, and position your car so that you can complete the exercise safely and correctly. You should then look carefully all around and reverse behind the parked car. If there is no car to the rear of the space, you will need to use your imagination and pretend that one is there.

You should make a point of practising this before you take your test and, in particular, ensure that you can judge your distance from the kerb without the help of a parked car behind on which to focus. You should finish the exercise stopped parallel, and reasonably close, to the kerb.

113

Reverse parking into a parking bay

At driving test centres with off street parking you may be asked to carry out a reverse park into a parking bay. This may be done at the start or the end of the test. If it is at the start of the test you will be asked to drive forward either to the left or to the right and then re-park your car in one of the bays keeping within the white lines. If the exercise is to be carried out at the end of the test the examiner will tell you to drive into the Centre car park and reverse park into any convenient bay.

It is important that you act in the same way as you would when parking in a car park. Do not try to reverse from a right-angle position. Drive your car forward level with the bay into which you want to park and then, depending on space, draw forward at an angle to either right or left so that the back of your vehicle is pointing towards the bay which you want to use. Make sure that you check it is safe before swinging to either right or left.

Then reverse into the bay and try to finish up within the white lines and with the whole of the car within the box.

While reversing it is acceptable to have a quick glance out of the offside window but you must not hang your head out of this side and neglect all-round observation. The secret of success in this exercise is to keep the car under control and moving slowly and keep looking all round the vehicle

– Watch out for oncoming traffic before you swing the front wing out to park.

Examiner tips

The examiner will expect you to:

– Reverse accurately into a parking bay

– Or reverse into a space of about two car lengths for the on-road manoeuvre.

The examiner will also be looking to see that you:

– Take all-round observation

– Stop within the parking box if it is a bay

– Stop reasonably close to the kerb if it is on-road

– Do not get too close to any other parked vehicles

– Do the whole exercise under control.

Common problems and reasons for failure

Candidates often try to reverse into the bay at right angles instead of drawing forwards at an angle and trying to reverse back as straight as possible.

Looking out of the right-hand window to see the white lines at the expense of all-round observation.

Turning the steering wheel too much – generally less is better.

Trying to do the exercise too quickly and losing control.

If the exercise is going badly wrong, don't wait, pull forward and correct the steering.

With an on-road reverse park candidates often stop too close to the car at the start of the exercise, making life very difficult.

Observations are often too late. The steering is turned to bring the rear end in. Invariably you look after the front end has swung out, blocked the road and forced a bus driver to brake, possibly leaving the passengers with neck problems.

Some people think the on-road reverse park exercise will always be done between two parked cars, which it is not.

– The secret of success in this exercise is to keep the car under control and moving slowly, until you're parked in the centre of the bay.

Pass Your Driving Test

Section 17

Road positioning and lane discipline

This section covers where you should position your car during normal driving. We have already been over in some detail where you should be on the approach to junctions and roundabouts. Right at the beginning you learnt how far from the kerb you need to be once you have moved away from the side of the road. Now you are going to expand your knowledge on this a little more.

Keeping to the left

In this country we drive on the left-hand side of the road. That sounds obvious, but actually if you bear that fact in mind it avoids confusion. So, the basic rule is to keep to the left except when overtaking or turning right.

Don't drive too close to the centre of the road. Doing so reduces the safety gap between you and oncoming traffic. Don't drive too close to the kerb. The bumps and drains in the gutter make steering control difficult. More importantly, you will be too close to pedestrians and have less time to react if they step into the road.

Generally speaking, you should be about a metre from the kerb. This is very flexible because on some narrow roads, a metre could mean you were crossing the centre line.

– In this country we drive on the left.

Traffic ahead may turn right. Be ready to go through on the left if there is room. After passing obstructions in the road

– Driving too close to the kerb can be dangerous to pedestrians and the drains can make steering control difficult.

– Use your judgement on narrow roads – being the proper metre from the kerb or edge may put you over the centre line.

return to the left. Do not weave in and out of frequent obstructions. Maintain a steady course. As far as lanes are concerned, you should:

– Drive in the middle of your lane

– Select the lane for the direction you intend to take

– Watch out for filter lanes at traffic lights.

Because we drive on the left, you should aim to take the lane closest to the left for the direction in which you want to go. For example, imagine you are approaching a major set of lights and wish to turn right. There are five lanes on the approach. One has a turn left arrow, the next two have straight-ahead arrows and the next two have right-turn arrows. You should select the left-hand lane of the two right-

hand lanes. In this way, once you have turned right you will finish up in the left-hand lane of the new road.

Examiner tips

The examiner will expect you to:

– Keep to the left normally

– Avoid weaving in and out between parked cars

– Obey lane markings.

The examiner will also be looking to see that you:

– Select the appropriate lane in good time

– Use the MSM routine.

– At road junctions with several lanes, choose the left-most lane in order to end up on the left after making the turn.

– Watch out for filter lanes, because they may be the only possibility to make a turn. If you're stuck, carry on and find another way.

Common problems and reasons for failure

Driving too close to the kerb – this would constitute a few centimetres for long periods or within 30 centimetres if there are pedestrians, particularly children, on the footpath. Both would be a fail.

Too far from the kerb would be a fail if it causes oncoming traffic problems. A few centimetres too far out would not cause failure unless it was taking the car over the centre lines and it was done throughout the test or exceeded 15 driver faults.

Problems with lanes: straddling or moving from lane without good reason. If other traffic was inconvenienced it would be an immediate fail.

– Driving too close to the kerb near children could warrant a failure.

Section 18

Passing stationary vehicles

When you first start learning to drive you will probably be driving up and down a deserted road with no people, no parked cars, no oncoming traffic. You may think, 'What a doddle, I can do this with my eyes closed.' If you do think this, you will be in for a shock when you drive on a normal road with parked cars, traffic and people.

When you are driving around town, there are very few roads where you will not have to pass stationary vehicles. Cars will be parked in most side roads; even on main roads, delivery vehicles and buses will be stopped at the side of the road. You must allow plenty of room when passing stationary vehicles.

You have already learnt how to deal with stationary vehicles in an earlier section on meeting traffic. You should look well ahead to spot any vehicles parked that might force you to change direction. Remember to consider the width of the road and the space available. Use the MSM routine. Check behind to see if it is necessary or safe to give a signal, and bear in mind that you can use your position as a signal. A gradual change of course is far safer than driving right up to the vehicle and swerving out at the last moment.

There might not be enough room for you to pass the obstruction because of an oncoming vehicle. So slow down, and be prepared to stop.

Where possible, allow at least a car door's width between you and parked cars. If you can't do this, slow down. Where there is less space, you need less speed to allow you more time to react should someone open a car door. Look for people sitting in the driver's seat, but remember that you cannot look into every parked car, so leave enough room anyway. Be prepared to stop if a stationary vehicle moves off.

Another reason for leaving a car door's width between you and parked cars is that a child could run out into the road. Look for feet under the cars and, again, be ready to stop.

Watch out for a cyclist who may pull out around a parked car without looking or stopping. And watch out for people coming out in front of a bus at a bus stop.

Examiner tips

The examiner will expect you to:

– Allow, if possible, the width of a car door.

The examiner will also be looking to see that you:

– Look out for doors opening, vehicles pulling away, children and pedestrians stepping out.

Common problems and reasons for failure

You could fail because of the speed you go through a gap. Sometimes there is no space to leave the correct gap and you would have passed if you had gone through slower.

You will not fail for reducing the gap, provided that it is not down to centimetres.

Pass Your Driving Test

Section 19 — Pedestrian crossings

Pedestrians, as you will have noticed, can't move as fast as cars. And yet they need to share the roads with all the vehicles on them and, ideally, want to be able to cross from one side of a road to the other without being flattened.

Drivers are also pedestrians

The volume of traffic on today's roads means that, as pedestrians, people often have considerable difficulty crossing anything but a quiet side road in safety. When we drive, we are often in a hurry and we can easily forget that when we are pedestrians we are no less pressed for time.

As both drivers and pedestrians we make mistakes, especially when we are in a rush. But when you drive, you are to a certain extent protected by your car. A minor accident is likely to damage your car, but not you, the driver. As a pedestrian you have no such protection, and the slightest bump with a car can, and often does, cause serious injury.

Pedestrian crossings are provided to help people cross the road safely. With few exceptions, even the most experienced driver is still a pedestrian at times. So it makes sense to ask yourself what you expect drivers to do when you wish to use a crossing. You expect them to show consideration and to slow down or stop to let you cross. You may expect this, but you're unlikely to depend on it happening. You are probably very careful when you try to cross the road on any type of crossing. Most of us realise, after a few near misses, that many drivers simply do not seem to see us or, if they do, seem to ignore our safety. Before you take your driving test, you may find it useful to act out the part of a pedestrian. Find a busy crossing and cross the road several times in both directions. Make a note of the drivers who seem to slow down and stop with ease, those who see you and are too late, and those who seem not to notice you at all. Then when you drive again, consider the advice that follows, and you should never have trouble giving way in good time.

There are several types of pedestrian crossings, which fall into two categories: uncontrolled and controlled.

– Make a note of drivers who see you and stop, and those who don't.

1 Uncontrolled crossings: these are zebra crossings and are referred to as uncontrolled because there are no lights or traffic controllers telling either drivers or pedestrians to stop.

2 Controlled crossings – a list follows:

Controlled crossings

Pelican

This stands for Pedestrian Light Controlled crossing. As a pedestrian, you push a button to change the signals. When the lights are red, a steady green-figure signal appears telling you that you may cross. When the green figure starts to flash it warns you that the lights are about to change and that you should not start to cross.

As a driver, on your approach you will see traffic lights and zigzag lines. The sequence of lights differs from that of lights controlling traffic at a junction, in that it includes a flashing amber instead of red and amber together.

When the amber light is flashing you must give way to any pedestrians still on the crossing, but you can drive on if the crossing is clear.

Toucan

This stands for Touch Controlled crossing. Toucans have the dual purpose of stopping the traffic for both pedestrians and cyclists. As a pedestrian, you operate them in the same way as a Pelican crossing.

When driving, you will see zigzag lines and lights on approach, but the sequence of lights is the same as at a set of traffic lights. Where you notice cycle routes, you should be prepared to see a Toucan crossing.

Puffin

This stands for Pedestrian User Friendly Intelligent crossing. Once again, you push a button to change the signal if you are a pedestrian. As a driver you will see zigzag lines on the approach. Puffins operate with an infra-red scan that holds the lights on red for as long as there is somebody on the crossing. As with the Toucan, there is no flashing amber light. They are most commonly found away from busy pedestrian areas.

Puffin crossings are of considerable benefit to drivers because they reduce unnecessary hold-ups in the flow of traffic. For example, at Pelican crossings, a pedestrian may push the button, see the road is clear, and cross before the signal changes to red. Any driver coming toward the crossing at that point still has to stop at the red light for no purpose; whereas, at a Puffin crossing, with the pedestrian having crossed safely, the sequence is electronically cancelled and the light stays on green.

School-crossing patrol

The 'lollipop person' is a familiar sight to most of us. A handheld sign on a pole stating 'Stop Children' tells drivers that they must stop. You will often see an earlier sign, 'School Patrol', which warns you that there is a school-crossing patrol ahead operating at certain times of the day. Amber lights may also flash with this sign when children are being supervised as they cross the road.

Uncontrolled crossings
Zebra crossings

This type of crossing has been around the longest. Its name is associated with the black and white stripes that mark the road. As a pedestrian, you stand there at the edge of the pavement, looking expectant and hoping the traffic will stop. When a vehicle on your side of the road does stop, you still exercise caution – another vehicle may overtake the one that has stopped for you, and the traffic on the other side of the road may still be oblivious to your presence. It means thousands of near misses, raised blood pressure and pumping hearts, but also a worse scenario – real accidents.

So how should you approach a zebra crossing when you are driving?

The first thing you need to do is to identify that there is a crossing ahead of you. You do this by looking for clues.

 There might be an advanced warning sign, usually if the crossing is coming up around a bend or over the brow of a hill. If you are in a pedestrian area, such as near shops, you should be checking for crossings anyway. Look for the flashing yellow beacons, zigzag lines and black and white stripes of the crossing itself. Try to spot them as early as possible. As soon as you have identified that you are approaching a crossing, you need to decide whether or not it is a hazard. Two things make a crossing a hazard:

– Either you can see pedestrians on or around the crossing

– Or you cannot see both sides clearly because of an obstruction.

A parked car or lorry, pedestrians, a tree, or a queue of oncoming traffic may obscure your view. You may not be able to see both sides of the crossing until you are nearly on top of it. If you can't see, you have no way of knowing if anyone is about to cross.

If the crossing is a hazard, you need to start the hazard routine: Mirror, Signal, Manoeuvre (MSM). Check in your mirrors the position and speed of any following vehicles and decide whether or not you need to give a signal. The signal will usually be your brake lights, and the earlier you start to brake gently, the more warning you give to the drivers behind you.

Nowadays, arm signals tend to be out of fashion, but this is one situation where a slowing-down arm signal can be particularly useful, especially if you are the leading vehicle approaching the crossing. This signal does three things. It warns traffic behind and oncoming traffic of your intention to slow down or stop. It also lets the pedestrians – who cannot see your brake lights – realise that you are giving way so they are more likely to cross sooner and with more confidence, thus reducing your delay to a minimum.

The manoeuvre is really about adjusting your speed, which needs to be slow enough to be able to stop safely should you need to do so. You <u>must</u> give way if someone is on the crossing, and you <u>should</u> give way if someone wants to use the crossing. You may be able to slow down and time your arrival for when the crossing is clear.

If you need to give way at a crossing, make sure you stop behind the line and not on the crossing itself. Avoid beckoning people across the road. Let them make up their own minds about whether it is safe to step into the road or not. You might make a mistake. As soon as it is safe, you should check your mirrors and move off.

The zigzag lines are there to protect pedestrians. You may not park within the area marked out by zigzag lines, thus ensuring that drivers have a good view of the crossing on the approach. And you may not overtake a moving vehicle on the approach to the crossing within the zigzag lines, or the leading vehicle that has stopped to give way to someone on the crossing.

Give a thought for the poor pedestrians and try not to scare them by edging forward or revving your engine while they are crossing. If you are in a queue of stationary traffic you should avoid obstructing the crossing with any part of your car.

The approach to the controlled crossings is basically the same. They should always be treated as a hazard: someone might have pressed the button earlier and the lights could still change to red, even though as you approach it appears that no one wants to use the crossing. As you near any green light try thinking 'Stop'. This does not necessarily mean slowing down. If the lights were to change to red, you would be expecting it. You would react faster than if you had been hoping the lights would not change, or thinking 'Go'.

– Don't wave pedestrians across the road. You might make a mistake and wave them into the path of an overtaking vehicle whose driver hasn't seen the pedestrians beginning to cross.

In summary, here are a couple of suggestions that can help you avoid getting caught out:

First, if you spot pedestrians crossing early enough, you can reduce your speed sufficiently to make sure that they have finished crossing before you get there. It is the people walking along the pavement near to the crossing who can catch you out. By the time they reach the crossing you will be much nearer. Perhaps they will cross, or push the button at a Pelican. Unless you have reduced speed a little, you may be too late to stop or have to brake harshly. So, anticipate the possibility, adjust your speed as needed, and be ready.

Second, at some Pelican crossings the lights change almost immediately a pedestrian pushes the button. So, once again, don't look just at the lights, look for pedestrians who might be about to push the button.

Examiner tips

The examiner will expect you to:

– Demonstrate consideration and courtesy for pedestrians

– Stop at pelican, puffin and toucan crossings if the lights are red

– Give way to pedestrians at pelican crossings if the lights are flashing amber

– Slow down and stop at zebra crossings if anyone is crossing or waiting to cross.

The examiner will also be looking to see that you:

– Control your speed on approach to pedestrian crossings

– Move off, after looking carefully to ensure it is safe.

Common problems and reasons for failure

Faults at pedestrian crossings tend to result in a fail. Most faults occur because you are not looking far enough ahead, the crossing comes on you at the last minute and you panic or take the wrong action.

Many people wrongly believe that you must pull up if someone is walking towards the crossing. They usually fail here for slamming on the brakes.

A similar problem can occur if you stop at a split crossing with a central island, with pedestrians only on the other half.

Approaching too fast is often a failing.

Plus points can be gained by giving a slowing-down arm signal. This is not often used but is always a welcome sight. Normally, not giving an arm signal would not cause failure unless there was a vehicle hammering up behind.

Section 20

Selecting a safe place to stop

Looking for somewhere legitimate to stop is not really too difficult provided you know what is behind you and plan well ahead. Once you have spotted a suitable place, you only need a confirming glance in your mirror to decide on whether to signal or not and can then slow down to assess the situation. This section contains the points to bear in mind.

Think before stopping

You should not park or stop, even for a few moments, in any place where you might cause danger or inconvenience to other road users.

When you are taking your driving test you will be asked on several occasions to pull up on the left at a convenient place because the examiner may wish to give you the instructions for one of the set exercises, like the emergency stop.

Remember that it sometimes may not be safe to stop immediately. Always check your mirror first, see if there is anyone close behind, and decide if a signal will be necessary. Pull up close to the edge of the road. Don't stop where you will make it difficult for others to see clearly, such as at or near a road junction.

Don't stop where it would make the road narrow, such as opposite another stationary vehicle. Don't stop where it would block an entrance, such as a driveway. Don't stop where it could cause danger, especially at or near a school entrance.

Every time you park thoughtlessly you put other people's lives at risk. You will have noticed, even as a pedestrian, some of the problems that drivers cause by stopping or parking in dangerous or unsuitable places.

The man on his way to work who parks on the corner to buy his paper risks causing an accident. The mother who collects her child from school and double parks in order to avoid a walk with the baby creates an equal danger.

When you think you have chosen a safe place, before you secure the car or switch off the engine, have a look around you. If you think being where you are could cause an inconvenience, or worse a danger, to someone else, move away and find somewhere better.

Examiner tips

The examiner will expect you to:

– Stop where you will not obstruct the road or cause a hazard

– Stop near to the edge of the road.

The examiner will also be looking to see that you:

– Do not cause danger or inconvenience to other road users when you stop.

Common problems and reasons for failure

Parking across someone's drive would normally be marked as a driver fault.

'Pull up at a convenient place on the left please,' means you pick the safe place and you do not have to stop immediately.

Section 21

Awareness and anticipation

Awareness means being awake to what is going on around you. It doesn't take a genius to work out that if you don't know what's happening, you're in big trouble when driving a car. If you want to drive a car safely you have to be aware for the whole of the time. That means you must concentrate only on the task of driving and you, along with everyone else, are likely to find this difficult.

Seeing is not always knowing

Most of us can focus all our energy and attention on a difficult task, but we can rarely sustain this level of concentration for more than a few minutes at a time. We are easily distracted. We tire quickly and part of our attention wanders to another problem. Because of this, drivers make mistakes and so do pedestrians, especially the very young and the elderly. Two out of every three pedestrians killed or seriously injured on the roads are either under 15 or over 60.

Anticipation is a form of guessing, but fortunately not quite so prone to error as guessing what numbers will come up in next week's National Lottery draw. Anticipation is guessing what will happen but based on reasons and on past experience. It means working out and judging what could possibly happen on the road ahead well before you get there. It means assessing what might happen as well as what actually is happening, and having a plan of action for every possible and actual problem that arises. Anticipation means not being caught out by the unexpected as well as being ready for what you thought was most likely to happen.

The earlier you can spot a possible problem, the easier you will be able to deal with it safely. You can avoid the need for a sudden action, such as harsh braking, that could endanger yourself and others.

As soon as you spot a potential problem, you must decide what action you need to take, and then respond as necessary. The faster you are travelling, the less time you have in which to do this. You will often need to reduce your speed simply to give yourself more time to think. As you drive along, you must stay alert and be looking well ahead continually and all around for any possible problems that may arise. Every time your vision is restricted or your space is reduced, slow down and give yourself more time to look and think and act.

This may all sound sensible and easy but there is rather more to it than meets the eye. And your eyes are the key to anticipation.

– Anticipation means never having to say sorry about the unexpected.

– As soon as you spot a potential problem, you must decide what action you need to take.

Your eyes can easily deceive you. This is partly because we all bring experience to what we see, and sometimes this causes us to see what we expect to see, and not what is actually there or happening. You have to do more than just look, you have to make meaning of what you see; that is, decide what is going to happen and whether it matters to you.

A driver ahead may be signalling left. Past experience suggests the car will turn left at the next junction and that is what you usually expect. But the driver may have simply left the signal on by mistake, or intend to park on the left. The driver may change their minds but not their signal, or not know left from right. You can get caught out.

You also have a problem because nobody can look and take in everything they see. The more you try to see at once, the less accurately you make sense of it all. On the other hand, if you focus all your attention on one thing, you tend not to see the other events happening around you.

133

The only solution is to learn to select what is important for you to see. A later section of this book – The five habits – explains a way of driving that helps you develop your ability to select what is important, make meaning of it and react safely. In the meantime, here are some examples of when awareness and anticipation can be a lifesaver. Consider the part they play in your driving test.

How to predict

When you take your driving test, your examiner will look to see how well you judge what other road users are going to do. Examiners have reason to be anxious, because if you turn out not to be ready for this they may have to take action.

Pay particular attention to the most vulnerable road users such as pedestrians, cyclists and motorcyclists.

Slow down anywhere near children who are playing and take extra care near schools.

Drive slowly past ice-cream vans and look carefully for the child who may run out. A ball in the road may be followed by a child.

Because children can be excitable, you have to learn to predict their possible actions and be ready for anything. If you see a child on one side of the road and more children on the other, consider whether they might be friends. Use your

– Drive slowly past an ice-cream van in case a child might run out from behind it.

imagination and ask yourself what could happen. The sudden recognition between them, a hasty wave, and any thoughts of the Green Cross Code are instantly forgotten – no looking, no thinking, just a frantic dash across the road to say hello. By continually asking yourself questions like this, you stay alert and learn to predict the unpredictable.

When you turn left or right, give way to pedestrians who are crossing the road. But do more than that. Look for the ones with their backs to you who are nearing the junction. Why should you expect them to glance over their shoulder and see you? Most of them won't. They'll step straight into the road, see you at the last minute and, if lucky, leap back onto the pavement in fright.

Be patient with the elderly and allow them time. Sound your horn to warn, but never to rebuke.

Watch out for pedestrians who don't look carefully when it is windy or raining. Ask yourself, would you risk raising your umbrella to look around if you thought the wind might blow it inside out? Probably not. You might just keep your head down, all thoughts on getting home, and hasten across the road. You can predict the unpredictable.

Give cyclists plenty of room. A cyclist who glances over the right shoulder may well intend to turn right in front of you. Watch out for motorbikes and cyclists when turning left. Use your nearside door mirror to spot them. Watch out for the bike that squeezes through the gaps in the traffic. Bear in mind that bikes are small and hard to see. Look twice and be sure.

Keep asking yourself, 'What's the nuttiest thing you can imagine that any of these other people sharing the road with you might do next?' Do that and you will very rarely ever be

caught out by the unexpected. You will have learnt to predict the unpredictable.

So, try to concentrate and stay aware all the time you are driving. Make use of the road signs and road markings to assess what lies ahead. Look all around for possible problems, and reduce speed when your vision is restricted or when your space is reduced.

That way you will avoid accidents, stay safe, and give your passengers a comfortable and confident drive. Don't forget that when you take your driving test, the examiner is your passenger.

– Keep asking yourself, 'What is the nuttiest thing you can imagine that any of these other people sharing the road with you might do next?'

By giving a comfortable ride that avoids harsh or late braking, you demonstrate that you are fully in control and that you are anticipating problems in good time. As a result, your chances of passing the test increase enormously.

Examiner tips

The examiner will expect you to:

– Be aware of other road users throughout your test

– Sensibly assess what other road users are about to do

– Predict how you will be affected by what they do

– Act on what you see or predict safely and in good time.

The examiner will also be looking to see that you:

– Demonstrate not only awareness of other road users but also show consideration for their safety

– Take special care not to endanger pedestrians particularly the elderly, the disabled and the very young as well as cyclists, motorcyclists and people in charge of animals.

Common problems and reasons for failure

Awareness and anticipation are needed for every driving task.

If an examiner has nowhere else to mark a fault, it goes under this heading.

Because anticipation – or rather the lack of it – is behind most faults, this one is often used when the examiner cannot think of anywhere else to mark it and it is generally a fault that will result in you failing.

Section 22   After the test

Your big day has come and gone. You have finished your driving test and are parked back near the test centre. The moment of truth has arrived and in that moment of tension, the examiner will deliver your fate and tell you whether you have passed or failed.

If you follow the advice offered in this book, and only take your test when your instructor tells you that you are ready, you should have little trouble passing at the first attempt.

Pass or fail?

When you pass your driving test, your examiner will ask you for your driving licence, and will give you a Pass Certificate. You should send this certificate to DVLA Swansea when you apply for your full licence.

You will also be given a copy of the Driving Test Report. This shows any faults that have been marked during the test. The idea behind this is to make you aware of any weaknesses in your driving, so that as you drive about and gain experience, you can make a conscious effort to improve on them.

If you fail, the examiner will give you a Statement of Failure, which will include a copy of the Driving Test Report. This will show all the faults that the examiner has marked during your test. The examiner will also spend a few moments explaining to you why you have failed.

After the test, it is strongly recommended that you discuss your Driving Test Report with your instructor. Your Approved Driving Instructor will be able to provide more information about the points raised in the report, and help you to understand exactly what went wrong.

If you fail, you will probably feel pretty fed up. Whatever you do don't give up. Your best bet is to apply for another test date straight away. Remember that every test centre has a waiting list of people wishing to take tests. This varies from one test centre to another, but is never likely to be less than five or six weeks.

It is best not to leave a gap before continuing your lessons and practice

– After the test, it's recommended that you discuss your Driving Test Report with your instructor.

sessions. The longer you wait, the more you will slip back, so follow your instructor's advice and book a course of lessons to take you up to your next test.

Your instructor will work with you to sort out your faults, but will also try to improve all aspects of your driving before you take another test.

Do not make the mistake of only practising the faults marked on your last test. If you do, you are likely to find that you fail on a different item the next time.

A word of warning. Even if you pass, don't drive away from the test centre yourself. Let your instructor drive for you. Your concentration will not be at its best and you may be far too excited to think clearly. Think positive – you've passed. You are now legally entitled to rush off home, rip off your L-plates and drive off in your car all on your own, without any supervision.

your car improves very quickly. Please be careful, because it is easy to develop a false sense of security. You no longer stall or have problems steering and so on. Everything seems to come naturally, without you having to think about it. So it can be all too easy to think that this has made you a good driver. But if your ability

– Don't become over-confident – you are at your most vulnerable in the first two years.

to look, spot problems early, assess risks and act sensibly does not also develop, you are likely to get caught out.

Regardless of your age, you are at your most vulnerable during the first few years of driving. In fact, an alarmingly high proportion of people have an accident during this period.

Driving on your own

You are likely to find that driving on your own is both exciting and a little nerve-wracking at first. If you keep practising the skills you have been taught, you should find that your ability to control

139

– There is no legal requirement to work towards an advanced driving test, but it can prove to be a rewarding experience.

For your own safety and that of other people, keep working at improving your driving once you have passed the test, but also take sufficient additional professional tuition.

At BSM you will find a team of Approved Driving Instructors who have been specially trained to provide expert help with post-test training. Short courses are available on night driving and motorway driving, and you will find both topics covered in later sections of this book.

A number of insurance companies may now be prepared to give you a discount on your insurance premium if you undertake a recognised course. The discount can often be more than the cost of the course, so you have little to lose and much to gain.

BSM offers a course called Risk Awareness, which is specifically tailored to the needs of the newly-qualified driver. Alternatively, many BSM instructors are registered to teach Pass Plus, a scheme developed by the Department of Transport. You can obtain details of these courses from any BSM Centre.

A note of caution. The content and purpose of post-test training for newly-qualified drivers should not simply be more of the same that you experienced as a learner. Not all instructors understand this, and you can be disappointed easily at learning nothing new. The best courses, like the BSM Risk Awareness course, pay little attention to your physical driving skills, but instead set out to develop your risk perception and reduce your personal risk level when driving.

In the next section some of the ways in which you can achieve this are explained.

Finally, you may in the future consider working towards an advanced driving test. There is no legal requirement to do so, but most people who have taken these tests have found the experience both pleasant and rewarding. Your local BSM Centre will be pleased to explain these advanced tests in more detail, and to give advice to you about the training you need to achieve the required standard.

Section 23

You and your car

Once you have passed your driving test and have become the proud owner of your first car, you will have to start dipping into your pockets and spending lots of money. Apart from anything else, you will become responsible for making sure that it is properly taxed, insured and tested.

Buying a car of your own

Most people do not start their driving career by buying a new car. They are far more likely to buy a second-hand one, and care is needed to ensure that what you buy is a sensible purchase in relation to the price you can afford. Unless you have mechanical knowledge, it is worth paying an expert to assess your intended purchase. Some motoring organisations like the RAC offer this service, which can save you much worry and helps take the risk out of buying second-hand.

However boring it is, always read your car handbook and stick to the manufacturer's recommendations. Have your car serviced at regular intervals and keep a record of any work done.

You will need to ensure that your car is always in a good roadworthy condition. Many people have a fear of breaking down. You can reduce this risk enormously if you take the following advice:

Daily checks

Walk round your car and look for obvious problems – flat tyres, damage to lights, loose trim, etc.

Make sure everything carried in the car is secure, and put loose items in the boot or glove compartment.

Make sure the windscreen and windows are clean. After you drive off, check that your brakes are working properly as soon as you safely can.

– Ensure that what you buy is a sensible purchase in relation to what you can afford.

Weekly checks

Think of the word POWER to help you remember what you should check:

– P is for petrol – or diesel. Make sure you have enough fuel for your journey. Allow extra in case you get caught in a traffic jam.

– O is for oil. Check the oil level and top it up if necessary. Check the brake fluid level, and also the clutch fluid, which may be in a separate container. If the oil pressure or brake warning lights come on while you are driving, stop as soon as you safely can and get help.

– W is for water. Check the radiator, or expansion tank, for the coolant level. Do this when the engine is cold. If it is hot, scalding water may spray over you as you remove the cap. Top up the windscreen washer bottle(s).

– E is for electrics. Make sure all the lights and indicators are working. Get someone to help you check the brake lights. Keep spare bulbs in the car so that you can carry out a quick roadside repair. If you take your car abroad, this is usually a legal requirement. Check that the battery connections are tight and clean. Top up the battery with distilled water if necessary.

– R is for rubber. Make sure your tyre treads are well above the minimum legal limit, and that there are no cuts or bulges in them. Check the tyre pressures when they are cold. Remember to check the spare.

In addition:

– Make sure the fan belt is tight and not worn.

– Check the wiper blades and replace them if they start smearing the windscreen.

Most car breakdowns are the result of failing to follow these simple steps. If you do breakdown, membership of a breakdown organisation, such as the RAC, will take away much of your worry and stress.

– Belonging to a motoring organisation relieves stress in case of a breakdown.

Pass Your Driving Test

Section 24 — The five habits

The selection process a car driver needs in order to focus on the hazards of most consequence was detailed in section 21. There, it was suggested that our eyes deceive us – unable to take in everything, we miss or misinterpret things. The solution is to learn how to be selective about what we see. This section deals with the five driving habits that allow the development of risk perception.

Developing risk perception

Many people have developed the skill of risk perception. Mastering the five driving habits will help you to identify risk and help you respond to the risks you come up against. They have very little to do with your hands and feet and the control of the car and everything to do with linking what is going on inside your head with what is happening on the road. They are all about reading the road, being aware and being selective.

— The five habits are:

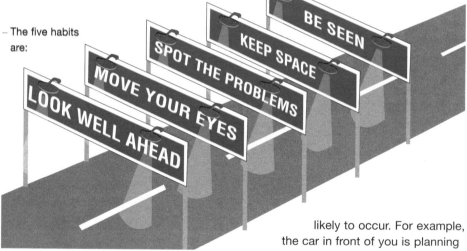

1 Look Well Ahead

Looking well ahead means deliberately raising your eyes above a benchmark halfway up the windscreen and looking well down the road. It's very easy to forget to look well ahead and instead concentrate on the car immediately in front of you rather than looking further ahead to see if there are any problems

These are all straightforward, and in fact you will have been putting them into practice throughout your driving so far. The difference is that you may not have been aware of it. What's important is to take them on board and make them habits. That means that you have to be actively and consciously using them all the time if they are going to be of any benefit at all to your driving.

likely to occur. For example, the car in front of you is planning to turn right. However, the driver forgets to signal and just starts to brake and slow down. You assume the driver is going to stop on the left and decide to overtake.

But if you were looking further ahead you would have collected more information. You would have noted the junction on the right, and thought, 'Brake lights, junction, I wonder.' This would have allowed you to include in your decision-making the possibility of the driver in front turning right.

Imagine you are driving along a road following three other cars, all of them travelling too close to each other. There is a side road on the left ahead of you all, from which a car is waiting to emerge, and there is oncoming traffic on the other side of the road. You cannot see the two cars at the front, the side road, the car waiting to emerge or the oncoming traffic because you are concentrating on the car in front of you.

The emerging car driver misjudges his gap and pulls out. The three cars in front of you slam on their brakes one after the other. Because they are travelling too close to each other they run into the backs of one another. You see the car in front of you do an emergency stop, realise you haven't the time to stop safely and swerve to the right in panic, straight into the oncoming traffic!

Not looking well ahead seriously reduces your options. Had you been looking well ahead, you would have seen the car emerge and could have started slowing down instantly, instead of leaving it until the car in front had to brake. You would also have seen that swerving to the right was not an available option. Instead, you could have slowed down a fraction to increase the gap between you and the car in front and so enlarged your space in which to stop safely.

Unless you look well ahead you have no means of deciding a sensible speed at which to drive. You must adjust your speed to fit the distance ahead that you are certain will stay clear. In places where a driver or pedestrian might appear and block your path you need to compensate by backing off the power, at least a little.

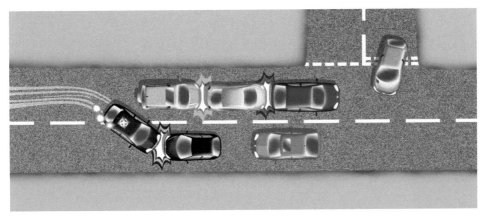

– Looking well ahead can prevent this kind of situation from developing.

2 Move your eyes

It isn't enough on its own to look well ahead because you will risk missing other hazards and problems. You also need to keep your eyes moving all the time into the near, middle and far distance, into your mirrors and, where necessary, the blindspots. Again, this needs to become a habit.

It is very easy when you are travelling for any length of time to find that your eyes become tired and are simply staring straight ahead. Moving your eyes helps you to stay alert. Whenever you allow your eyes to fix on anything for a while, the edges of your vision become blurred and you cease to detect movement. If you cannot keep your eyes moving, you are almost certainly getting tired and are in need of a break from driving.

Even alert, you cannot focus well on things at the edges of your vision unless you move your eyes. You may detect movement, but it would be blurred and you wouldn't, for example, see a child stepping out from between parked cars at the side of the road if you were looking exclusively straight ahead down the road.

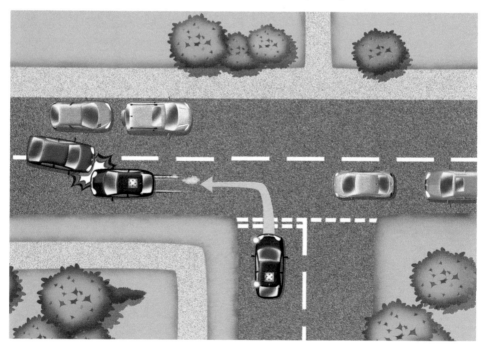

– It's essential to keep your eyes moving at all times, otherwise you might not view the parked cars seen in this example as a potential hazard. In traffic, the situation can change rapidly.

However good our eyesight may be, we are only capable of seeing things in clear focus in a narrow cone of central vision that is about 3° wide. We use this to look well ahead, but we catch movement out of the corners of our eyes. This is known as 'fringe vision'. Advanced drivers use fringe vision as a way of detecting problems. In older age fringe vision deteriorates, which means more eye movement is needed to keep up with changes happening around the car.

Classic accidents happen every single day on the roads because drivers do not keep their eyes moving. One of the most obvious examples occurs in emerging. You come up to the end of the road, intending to turn left. You see a steady stream of traffic coming from your right and watch it, looking for a safe gap. You see a gap. In order to emerge safely, however, you have to put your foot down or risk causing another driver to have to brake for you. You emerge and, as you turn your head to the left to look where you are going, you drive straight into a car coming towards you on your half of the road.

You hadn't moved your eyes to the left before deciding it was safe to go and so missed the fact that parked vehicles on the other side of the road forced any traffic coming from your left to steer around them, obviously putting them on your side of the road.

3 Spot the problems

The reason you need to be looking well ahead and moving your eyes is so that you can spot problems. Looking well ahead and moving your eyes every couple of seconds is hard work, but the more you look, the more you discover what there is to see. You need to be able to decide what, out of all the things you see, may cause you a problem.

In other words, you are using your mind as well as your eyes, not just to see problems that put you at risk, but to predict a possible risk before it becomes reality. This may be sounding familiar from the explanations in the 'Awareness and anticipation' section. The better you are at spotting risks either before or as they develop, the more time you have to take steps to reduce the possibility of an accident. Many accidents happen either because drivers fail to identify something as a problem, or because by the time they do it is too late to act.

Imagine that you are approaching a set of traffic lights on green. There is always the possibility that the lights will change to red before you get there. So you need to make a decision as to how you're going to deal with them. Consider the problems around you. You check your mirrors and see a car following too closely behind. Additionally, there is a car in the junction waiting to turn right across your path. The driver may decide that there is enough time to turn in front of you. This would be a serious problem if

– Many accidents happen because the driver fails to identify a problem, like not slowing for lights in wet weather with a car behind.

that driver had misjudged your speed and the size of the gap, and if he didn't take into consideration the time it would take you to slow down or stop with someone following so closely behind. Worse still, it's raining. So the roads are wet, which will naturally increase your overall stopping distance.

Spotting problems means adding all the things together that could possibly affect you, and then coming up with a solution. In this instance, the solution may well be to start slowing down immediately on seeing the lights, even though they are still on green.

4 Keep space

Trying to keep space on today's roads is no easy matter. As you drive, you need to achieve two aims that appear contradictory. You need to keep pace with traffic while keeping space from traffic.

Space around your car gives you time to look, think, spot risks and react. Space around your car gives you an escape route should anything go wrong, or should anyone else make a mistake. The smaller the space around you, the greater the risk you are taking. To keep risk to the minimum, think that less space should equal less speed.

Looking well ahead and moving your eyes allows you to foresee where your space will be reduced, and to spot space invaders before they cause you a problem. Tiny adjustments to your speed – by easing off the gas or covering the brake – let you keep as much space in front as you need, allowing you to time your arrival at dangerous situations and keep the safest possible position relative to other traffic on the road.

It is worth bearing in mind that, when you are driving, you only have three options available: you can change speed, you can change direction or you can give a warning signal. Space gives you the chance to keep all your options open for as long as possible.

– Birds never bump into each other – but humans do it all the time.

Far too many drivers believe themselves to be safe, despite the restricted space they are allowing themselves. There is a problem here, and it has a lot to do with the human competitive spirit. We find it extremely difficult to concede space. We feel that if we drive closer to the car in front, we will get to our destination quicker. We feel that if we leave even a tiny gap, someone would nip in and steal our space and that would hold us up.

Another aspect to this problem is that we really believe that because our reactions are fast we don't need the amount of space everyone tells us we do, and that our reactions are faster than anybody else's. This simply is not true. Compare flocking seagulls or stampeding antelope with humans. Even in excitement or panic, these creatures never bump into each other, but humans

on a crowded pavement are always knocking each other.

The fact is that at a walking pace, or perhaps a little faster, our reactions are poor. We are incapable of moving around at the speeds we were designed to move about at, without permanently crashing into someone else. And yet we think we can drive at speeds of up to 70mph without bumping into another vehicle. We can't, unless we give ourselves time to react, and that is what keeping space is all about.

5 Be seen

The danger of being hit by another vehicle or hitting a pedestrian is greatly increased if they cannot see that you are there or understand from your position or signals what you intend to do next.

151

Being seen is your means of communication with other road users. You cannot expect others to see you or even to use efficient seeing habits. You must make them see you, and even then you cannot entirely rely on them not to make a wrong move.

Clear communication with other traffic is essential. You need to know what others are doing or are about to do. You need to be clear about what to expect of them and what they expect of you. Many crashes are followed by cries of 'I didn't see him…' or 'I didn't think she would pull out!' In particular, these statements are common after junction or overtaking crashes. So do not assume another driver or pedestrian has seen you, or that other vehicles will stay put.

There are many ways of making yourself seen when driving. For example: lights, flashing lights, signals, brake lights, horn, making eye-to-eye contact, keeping out of other drivers' blindspots, fog lamps, position on the road.

This sets out for you the main points about each of the five habits. To get the best out of them, you need to learn how to use each habit, not in isolation but in conjunction with the others. You would also find it useful to keep practising them each time you go out and drive.

– There are many ways of making yourself seen when you're driving.

Section 25 # Night driving

Before you pass your driving test, you may well drive in the dark, especially if you have lessons during the winter months. Even if this is the case, you still need to think about the difficulties arising from driving at night that this section raises.

– Driving at night can be quite a strain.

General rules

The chances of being involved in an accident are greater in the dark than in daylight. You cannot see as far or as much at night, and you receive far less information about your surroundings.

It is harder to judge both speed and distance, and driving is more of a strain, particularly on the eyes. From dusk to dawn you must rely on lights to see and to be seen.

Driving at night can be a great strain on your eyes. As you get older, your eyesight may alter. Such changes tend to take place so gradually that you are unlikely to notice them. The only way you can be sure your vision is adequate is to have your eyesight checked regularly, preferably by visiting a qualified optician.

When you decide to drive in the dark, you need to bear in mind a number of points:

– Don't use sunglasses or tinted glasses at night – they reduce your vision

– Keep your windscreen clean – you will see better and be less dazzled by other vehicles' lights

– Check that all your lights are working and that they are clean and properly adjusted – the effectiveness of your lights is greatly reduced if they are dirty

– If you are tired – don't drive.

You should make sure that you can see and be seen by other road users. So it is best to use headlights on all roads. In towns where there is street lighting, use dipped headlights. Sidelights are not enough and make it difficult for other drivers and pedestrians to see that you are there.

– A clean windscreen will cut down on dazzle from other vehicles' lights.

– At night, stopping within the distance you can see to be clear means within what your headlights show.

Don't wait for others: at dusk, be the first to turn on your lights; at dawn, be the last to turn them off.

Night stopping distances

Section 10 outlined the need to exercise care in the use of speed and how you must be able to stop within the distance you can see to be clear. Remember that at night this means being able to stop well within the limits of your lighting.

On an unlit road, headlights on full beam allow you to see approximately 100 metres ahead and dipped headlights allow you to see about 40 metres ahead.

These figures are only approximations because the type of car you are driving, and the angle of the beam of light, alters the distance you can see with the headlights. But these figures should help you appreciate just how much less you can see in the dark than in the daylight.

Pedestrians and cyclists are hard to see in the dark. They don't always wear reflective clothing, and cyclists do not always have good working lights.

Cats' eyes, however, make driving on roads equipped with them much easier. They help you to follow the course of the road ahead as your headlights pick them out.

Dealing with other traffic

The lights of another vehicle usually tell you its direction of travel but little about its speed. Decide if you need to slow down and look for any obstructions in the road ahead.

Dip your headlights to avoid dazzling oncoming drivers. Do not dip so soon that you cannot see the road ahead. Do not stare at the oncoming headlights, but look slightly towards the left-hand edge of your dipped beams. Be ready to stop if necessary. Dip your lights earlier when going around a left-hand bend. Your headlight beams will sweep across the eyes of anyone coming towards you. If an oncoming driver fails to dip his lights and dazzles you, slow down and stop if necessary.

When you are following other vehicles at night remember that your headlights on full beam can dazzle the driver in front as much as they can an oncoming vehicle. It is really disorientating to be dazzled by the vehicle behind you, and it becomes quite impossible to focus properly on the road ahead when there is a bright light in your interior mirror filling your eyes. So dip your lights if you are following another vehicle and keep far enough back that your dipped beams fall clear of the rear window.

Extra care is needed if you overtake at night. It is much harder to judge space and distance and the speed of other vehicles in the dark. Dangers are far more likely to be hidden from view. You cannot see properly beyond the range of your headlights.

Bends or dips in the road may conceal parked or approaching vehicles. Cyclists and pedestrians may be hidden in the gloom.

If you need to warn of your presence at night, flash your headlights. It is illegal to use your horn when driving in a built-up area between the hours of 11.30pm and 07.00am.

There are no examiners' tips in this section, because driving tests only take place during the hours of daylight. It is up to you once you have passed your test to practise driving in the dark. It is especially difficult to cope when you are on an unfamiliar, unlit road that bends all over the place and the driver behind is so close that you are being dazzled by the car lights. Let the driver pass if you get the chance. It's much safer than feeling pushed to go too fast.

– After passing your test, it's up to you
  to practise night driving.

Pass Your Driving Test

Section 26 Motorways

Learner drivers are not allowed on motorways, so unless you have passed your test by the time you read this section you have yet to experience what it is like to drive on one. Some new drivers find their first drive on a motorway pretty scary. If they are not prepared properly, and don't really know the rules very well, they can find the speed of other vehicles alarming and have little idea of what to expect or what to do. If you take account of the advice in the following pages, you will have no need to repeat their unfortunate and dangerous first experiences of motorway driving.

The reason for motorways

The Romans were probably the first people to think up the concept of motorways and put it into practice. They needed to shift lots of people and equipment over long distances from one place to another as quickly as possible. They didn't want their troops to arrive worn out, nor did they want to lose half of them on the way through unexpected attacks from hidden ambushes on the way ahead.

Their solution was to build roads unlike any before them: roads wide enough for fast-moving vehicles and soldiers to overtake slow-moving baggage carts and people; roads as straight as possible so that they could look well ahead and avoid the possibility of hidden ambush; roads with all the undergrowth on either side removed for clear long vision around the few bends; and roads with safe watering-holes, rest and refreshment areas at regular intervals along the route. The Romans conquered half the world and ruled it for centuries, partly because this strategy was so successful.

Our modern motorways were first designed with many of these concepts in mind (apart, perhaps, from the ambush bit). The solution to increasingly long road journeys was a system that would allow cars and freight to travel efficiently, quickly and safely by road. And so in the late 1950s the motorway building programme began, and a glance at any recent road map will show you the extent to which it has developed.

Motorways have solved some problems but have created others of their own; not least, the sometimes terrible accidents that are reported in the news media. In fact, motorways are the safest of all our

– Motorways were designed to solve all our transport problems.

at the wheel. You don't want to be one of them.

Moreover, with so few background clues, like the size of buildings, you can easily misjudge the speed and distance of other vehicles.

Our motorways are often as full of traffic as any town street, and many people drive on motorways as if they were driving on town streets. They leave the same sort of gap in front at 70mph, that they would leave when driving in town at 20 or 30mph.

roads. But when accidents happen, the speed and volume of traffic can often result in serious injury or death. Your statistical chances of being an accident victim on a motorway may be less than on other roads, but that is small comfort if you become one of the statistics.

Motorways are quite different from ordinary roads. For one thing, they are deliberately designed to be featureless environments. They are boring places! That's one of the problems. At one time it was thought that not having the usual distractions of traffic lights, shops and advertisement hoardings would make motorways safer roads. Unfortunately, this has produced a range of different problems that you will need to learn to cope with.

For one thing, you are likely to find it very difficult to stay alert when there is so little happening around you. People fall asleep

Like many drivers, you may feel nervous about using motorways. So far you may have had little or no training in driving at speed or overtaking. How many vehicles have you overtaken which were doing more than 30mph? This section outlines the main problems you are likely to face, and suggests the sort of actions you can take to help you stay safe.

– First time out, you may not know motorway rules very well.

Preparation

Safe motorway driving starts before you set out. You need to prepare for your journey. Why? Well, you are not allowed to stop on the motorway to read a map, or to have a little shut eye. If your car breaks down, there is no alternative transport and it is illegal to hitch a lift.

Once you are on the motorway there may be no way off for 10 or more miles and traffic jams can be 20 miles long. Fun places really, motorways. So, you need to think about you, your car and your route before you set off.

– You

You need to be feeling fit, alert and well rested. If you've been up half the night partying or rocking the baby, your concentration will not be at its best and you will need all of it.

– Make sure you're well equipped with everything your car will need on the journey.

– Your car

– Fuel, oil, water

Motorway speeds use these up quickly. Allow extra fuel for getting caught in traffic hold-ups.

– Brake fluid, tyres

Top brake fluid up to the full level. Check tyre pressures, including the spare. (Check your car's handbook for recommended tyre pressures for motorway driving.) Make sure you have a jack and all the other necessary tools for changing a wheel.

– Windscreens, washers, wipers

Check your washer bottle is full and the wiper blades are in good condition. Clean windscreens, windows and mirrors.

– Luggage

Make sure anything carried is secure.

– Your route

Check at which junction you will leave the motorway. Note the exit number. Your destination may not be listed on the sign. Many major towns are served by more than one exit. You need to check which exit best fits the part of the town you want to get to. Before long journeys, check the distances and availability of services. It is worth noting an alternative route in case of problems. Check weather and traffic conditions. Information can be obtained by phone, the internet, teletext or radio.

Joining a motorway

Motorway junctions are designed to enable you to join without causing problems to the traffic already on the motorway, which has priority. Your aim should be to time your entrance onto the main carriageway so that you blend safely into the traffic pattern.

Many junctions have downhill entry slip roads, which give you a good early view of the traffic. Your first look should be to the motorway ahead to check:

–   The speeds of vehicles already on the motorway

–   For any broken-down vehicles

–   For traffic hold-ups.

– Time your entrance onto the main carriageway so that you can blend safely into the traffic.

Next, look to see what drivers ahead are doing, and start glancing to your right to:

–   Look for gaps in the traffic

–   Check for drivers changing lanes

–   Judge how fast traffic is moving.

The early look will help you to plan your approach to joining the motorway. The slip road leads into an acceleration lane which runs alongside the main carriageway. This allows you to see clearly the traffic on the motorway and to spot and select a gap. It also allows you

161

– Many drivers leave it too late to look for a gap, hesitate, then join at too slow a speed.

to adjust your speed to that of the through traffic while still on the acceleration lane, so that you can move onto the main carriageway safely.

So that's what you want to achieve. The next question is: how do you do it?

Let's look at the problems you will encounter, and find some helpful solutions.

Other traffic may be on the slip road with you: cars overtaking, cars behind, traffic ahead getting bunched, cars stopping to wait for a gap in the left-hand lane. By keeping in the left-hand lane, you allow traffic to overtake and you can keep

track of it more easily. By staying well back from traffic joining ahead, you can reduce the risk of running into the back of them if they do have to slow down or stop. Many drivers leave it far too late to look for a gap, then hesitate on the acceleration lane, slow down and join at far too slow a speed. This causes bunching in through-traffic and sudden, unplanned lane changing as drivers try to get around the slower vehicle.

Accidents are frequently caused in this way. By looking early for a suitable gap, you can spot opportunities to join that might not be there a few moments later, either because the gap has passed you by or because someone else has taken it.

Begin looking as soon as you have a view of the main carriageway. If your attention is fixed on looking for a gap you may not see what other drivers are doing. Vehicles in front of you may have to slow down or stop before joining. Keep well back from the vehicle in front and take many short glances to look for a gap. This is safer than one long look, so keep moving your eyes all the time. You should aim to cause the least possible disruption to the traffic flow on the motorway.

Drivers who approach too fast have less time to spot a gap. If there isn't one, they either force their way in, disturbing the through traffic, or have to brake at the last minute and wait for a gap (both of which are potentially dangerous).

Keep to a moderate speed until you have selected a gap, then use the acceleration lane to build your speed to match the speed of traffic in the left-hand lane.

There may be a continuous line of traffic in the left-hand lane. Give a signal early so other drivers can see you more easily. Some drivers may move to the middle lane to let you join more easily.

There may be a vehicle immediately alongside you. Make a quick shoulder check just before you join, which will reveal a vehicle hidden in the blindspot, or possibly a vehicle in the middle lane moving back to the left-hand lane.

If you cannot join, it is best to slow and stop well before the end of the acceleration lane. The space left allows you to build up speed when there is a gap. But check your mirrors before

– If you signal early enough, drivers may move to the middle lane to let you join.

slowing down. Drivers behind may be looking the wrong way.

When you join, steer gently into lane and cancel your signal. Stay in the left-hand lane until your senses have adjusted to the higher speeds.

So remember, your aim is to time your entry onto the main carriageway to blend into the through traffic, which has priority.

- Keep clear of other drivers on the entry slip road

- Look early for a suitable gap

- Adjust your speed to match traffic in the left-hand lane

- Give a signal

- Make a quick shoulder check

- Steer gently into the left-hand lane

- Cancel the signal

- Stay in the left-hand lane until your senses have adjusted to the higher speeds.

Driving at higher speed

It is frequently said: 'Any fool can make a car go fast, but it takes an expert to stop it.' This somewhat pretentious comment does contain an element of truth, because when you double your speed your braking distance becomes four times greater.

The faster you drive, the further ahead you need to look in order to spot problems early. If you don't spot problems early enough you may not have time to react and prevent an accident.

On your driving test you are asked to do an emergency stop at around 20mph. You know the signal is coming. You know there is no actual danger, and you will have practised the exercise before. That is all it is, after all, an exercise. But many drivers have no real idea of how long it takes to stop a car being driven at 70mph in a real emergency, without any warning, after some hours driving and with their attention beginning to wander.

On a dry motorway it takes up to two seconds to react and start braking, plus at least six seconds to brake to a stop. (Six seconds is roughly equivalent to the 75 metres braking distance shown in the Highway Code.) So, it takes a total of eight seconds in order to stop. This means you need to be looking past the traffic immediately in front of you towards the point where the road vanishes out of sight. Motorways are designed to give you excellent visibility. You need to

practise looking well ahead and scanning the road in front of you for problems, gradually working back to your position.

LGVs (Large Goods Vehicles), coaches and other large vehicles may block your view ahead. If you can, change lanes to get a better view. If you can't, drop back so that you can see further ahead to allow yourself space to stop if the lorry stops suddenly for something you can't see.

When LGVs are overtaking, cars will have to funnel into the right-hand lane in order to overtake. This will cause following traffic to bunch up and slow down.

Try to look well ahead for situations like

– **Big lorries will dangerously restrict your view ahead if you follow too closely behind.**

this. In particular, watch out for lorries climbing hills where this problem often arises, and make any speed or lane changes early. Keep a look out for stationary or slow-moving traffic ahead. This often leads to drivers suddenly changing lanes to take the line that is moving the most freely.

Look well ahead for brake lights, hazard warning lights, indicators, emergency traffic signals and emergency vehicles. Give yourself time to slow down. Watch out for drivers invading your stopping space.

165

Sometimes you will see flashing amber lights up ahead and an advised speed limit sign. You may be tempted to ignore the sign like so many other drivers do. Perhaps the problem has been cleared, but nobody has yet turned off the sign. But relying on 'perhaps' is risky. An accident may be blocking the whole motorway. You may not be able to see the problem; the police patrol unit can. Just beyond the sign there could be a queue of stationary traffic.

So move to a lane on the left, if necessary, so that you can safely reduce your speed. Remember, your aim is to look well ahead and give yourself time to react to changes.

- At 70mph it takes up to eight seconds to react and brake to a stop

- Practise looking to the vanishing point and working back to where you are

- Look well ahead for lorries overtaking, particularly on hills

- Look well ahead for signs of traffic that may be slowing down

- React to road signs even though you cannot see the reason for them yet.

- Have a regular break to give your senses something else to do.

How speed deceives

When you are driving at high speeds, you are likely to be going faster than you think. Drivers often dangerously underestimate how fast they are travelling. The featureless motorway environment often makes this worse, particularly at night. Driving a vehicle which travels at speed effortlessly and noiselessly only adds to this. Check your speedometer regularly. You may find yourself speeding up to compensate for the feeling that you are going slower than you really are.

It's much harder to judge things accurately if you travel for long distances at the same speed without a break. Because this tends to have a numbing

effect, it's sensible to vary your speed. As an example, after a few miles at 70mph, drop down to 65mph for a while. Even 5mph makes a difference and keeps you more alert. Taking regular breaks at a services or somewhere off the motorway will give your senses something else to do. As a guide, take a 15-minute break about every 2–3 hours.

So always keep in mind that speed deceives, and remember to:

– Check your speedometer regularly

– Vary your speed from time to time

– Take regular breaks.

Judging the speed and distance of other vehicles

The question is: 'Can you judge speed and distance accurately?' The truth is most people can't. Yet this ability is vital to safe motorway driving. The car coming up behind you may be moving much faster than you are. One look in the mirrors will only give you a still picture of what is happening. It is only by taking second and subsequent glances that you can get any idea of the speed of the vehicle behind you and how long it will take to catch up to you.

Door mirrors are often made of convex curved glass. They give you a wide field of vision, but also make vehicles look smaller and further away than they really are. If you only use the door mirrors as a guide you might easily make a mistake and pull out when about to be overtaken.

Because the interior mirror is normally made of flat glass, it shows the size and distance of vehicles more realistically – but you can see less of the road behind. Looking in the interior mirror makes it easier to judge how far away vehicles are and how fast they are gaining on you.

Because of the way our eyes work, if you stare fixedly at one part of the traffic scene it makes it very difficult to judge someone else's speed.

For example, if you focus solely on the car ahead of you, the background tends to become vague and out of focus.

167

You should view the traffic ahead as part of a scene that includes bridges, signs, changes in road surface and other background features. These features are now distinct and can help you judge the speed of traffic ahead. Practise trying to assess the speed of following traffic in the same way.

So you should aim to get the 'big picture':

– See other vehicles as part of a huge roadway scene that includes all the background features

– Practise judging the speed of traffic ahead and how long you will take to reach it

– Practise judging the speed of traffic behind and how long it will take to reach you.

– The door mirrors can fool you as to the distance of vehicles coming up behind you.

Following at a safe distance

The problem of drivers following too closely has become almost legendary. It is the most common cause of accidents on motorways. Without a gap you do not have time to react, to slow down or to stop if others do. Leaving enough distance between you and the vehicle in front is one of the most important steps any driver can take to reduce the risk of accidents.

Drivers allow the same sort of separation distance on motorways as they do on ordinary roads. But remember, reaction times tend to be longer. You may recall the idea of leaving a gap of a metre for every mile per hour of your speed. But can you judge 70 metres?

You may recall that in section 11 how to use the 'two-second rule' was explained. Using a time gap is easier than trying to judge distances. This is so important that a reminder will not go amiss. What you do is simple. As the car in front goes past or under something, like a road sign or a bridge, say to yourself: 'One thousand and one, one thousand and two.' This takes about two seconds to say. If you go past the same point before you can finish saying this, you are too close. You can practise this when driving on non-motorway roads. Pick out any stationary object, like a pillar box or lamp post, and use the two-second rule. Try to watch the traffic well ahead so that you can see when it will be slowing down. This will enable you to start slowing down early, and so maintain a safe gap in front of you.

Drivers get frustrated. They harass drivers who are 'in their way'. They may drive up your exhaust pipe, flash their lights at you and weave from side to side in the traffic lane. Eventually they may be tempted to undertake (overtake you on the left) and cut back sharply in front of you. Don't speed up, but do move over and let them through as soon as it is safe to do so. Don't do this because they are right, but because your action will reduce the risk of an accident.

– You should aim to leave at least two seconds between you and the vehicle in front

– Watch changes in the traffic several cars ahead

– Move over and let the frustrated driver through.

– Note: Chevron-shaped markings are now in use on some sections of motorway, and are popular on busy sections of the French system. These make it easier to judge a safe following distance at a given speed limit. All you have to do is make sure that you can see two chevron markings between your car and the vehicle in front. So, car A is driving safely, car B is not.

Hard shoulder	Left-hand lane	Middle lane	Right-hand lane
Emergencies only. Never use the hard shoulder to overtake.	Use this lane unless overtaking. In an emergency it is much easier to reach the hard shoulder if you are driving next to it.	Use this lane to overtake traffic in the left-hand lane. You may stay in the middle lane if you are overtaking a line of slower-moving vehicles. This is safer than moving in and out repeatedly.	Use this lane to overtake traffic in the middle lane. Large Goods Vehicles (LGVs) and vehicles towing trailers are not allowed to use this lane if all three lanes are open.

Do not straddle lanes

Driving in lanes

Most motorways have three lanes in each direction, although some have only two and certain stretches of very busy areas have four. More lanes mean more traffic can flow. Faster traffic is not held up by slower vehicles, because in theory they can use the other lanes to overtake.
In practice, unless the lanes are used correctly, there is a lot of wasted space and drivers become frustrated. Using the lanes properly is an important part of safe motorway driving.

So, what are the rules?

You should normally overtake only on the right. But if traffic is moving slowly in queues, a different rule applies. It is then safer to keep pace with traffic in your lane, even if this means you are overtaking traffic on your right. Never move to a lane on the left to overtake. Many drivers do not know the rules; many deliberately break them.

So, these are the rules, and now here are some of the problems and some help to resolve them.

You will often see a driver trundling merrily along in the middle lane when there is no traffic immediately ahead. The driver should be in the left-hand lane, but perhaps can't be bothered. The question is: when should you move back to the left? If there is time to get over to the left and let some other traffic through before you need to get back out again, move over.

It is strongly advised that you do not become a lane hogger. For example, LGVs are not allowed to use the right-hand lane of a three-lane motorway. Lorry drivers get quite angry if you hold them up by hogging the middle lane. They will often drive within inches of your back bumper, which can be quite alarming and is certainly very dangerous. They may be wrong, but they're bigger than you. You risk getting squashed, so swallow your pride and move back to the left-hand lane and let them overtake. Even if you are doing 70mph you should still keep to the left. Let other drivers overtake you even if they will be exceeding the speed limit.

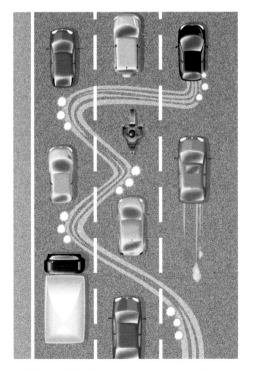

– Watch out for 'lane dodgers', especially in slower-moving traffic.

When the motorway is busy, queues form in each lane. 'Lane dodgers' move from lane to lane to try to move up the queue. Stay in lane. If your lane moves faster than the others, just keep in step with it, even if this means overtaking on the left. This is within the rules about traffic queues. But do watch for lane dodgers. The queue of traffic may be moving at 60mph. Because everyone is moving at roughly the same speed and in the same direction it doesn't feel as fast as that. Often drivers travel much too close together for their speed. Drivers in this situation are known as 'wolf packs'.

Keep pace with traffic in your lane, but keep space around you in case you have to slow down or stop. Other drivers may cut into your lane, so expect this and for your own safety drop back to open up space again.

So, obey the rules but use your commonsense. Try to make your main aim to move back to the left as soon as you safely can, letting drivers overtake if they wish even if they will be breaking the speed limit.

– Keep to the left unless overtaking

– In queues it is safer to keep pace with the traffic in your lane, even if this means you are overtaking traffic on your right

– Never move to a lane on the left to overtake.

171

Changing lanes

Lane changing is a skill you will need in many motorway situations: overtaking, roadworks, breakdowns, joining, leaving, where motorways divide, etc. Motorways allow you to see well ahead. This enables you to plan when to change lane so as to cause the minimum of disruption to the traffic flow. You should avoid waiting to the last moment to look for a chance to pull out around slower vehicles. This approach often means getting 'boxed in' by overtaking traffic and having to slow down and follow the slower vehicle.

Try to judge how quickly you are gaining on the one in front. Weigh up the situation behind and decide the best time to move out for overtaking. Signal before you move then take a quick glance to your right just to make sure there isn't a driver in your blindspot.

Drivers sometimes leave changing lanes to the last moment, either through lack of attention or through trying to get ahead of other drivers. Turning the wheel suddenly or sharply may cause loss of control, a skid, or even turn the car over.

Anticipate the need to change lane and make all your steering movements gentle. Make a lane change over a long distance. When you want to change lane, simply look well ahead to the centre of the next lane. By looking where you want to go your eyes can control your hands and you will steer gently into the new lane.

The main aim is to look well ahead and assess the need to change lane as early as possible. Try to judge how quickly you are gaining on the driver in front. Check mirrors, signal and check the blindspot before you move.

– Look well ahead to avoid getting 'boxed in' by overtaking traffic.

Roadworks

Roadworks are a fact of life and probably always will be. Many of our older motorways need repairing, and there are many schemes to widen existing motorways.

Roadworks often cause traffic jams, traffic jams cause delays and frustration, and frustration can lead to accident situations. Try to find out where major roadworks are causing delays and avoid them. If this is not possible, allow extra time and fuel for being stuck in the traffic.

Roadworks create additional dangers because they reduce the space and number of lanes available. Some roadworks will mean two-way traffic using one carriageway. This is the infamous contraflow system. These have compulsory speed limits and stay-in-lane rules. Some horrific accidents have occurred in these systems. So take extra

– **With advance planning, you may be able to find a route to avoid motorway roadworks.**

care. Slow down early, obey the speed limits and keep as much space as possible between you and other vehicles.

Where the number of lanes reduces from three to two or two lanes to one, many drivers leave it far too late to get into a lane that is open. They are queue jumping, but however much you might wish to see them stuck, it is never worth taking risks. Just be calm and let them in.

Bear in mind that lanes in roadworks can often be very narrow. You need full concentration when oncoming vehicles are only a few feet away.

– Look well ahead, and keep within the speed limit until you see a sign advising that the restriction is over

– Aim to find out where the roadworks are and, if possible, avoid them

– Let in the driver who leaves it late to get in lane

– Allow more time and fuel for your journey

– Concentrate on steering a steady course when driving in narrow lanes.

behind you. Unless you scan the mirrors frequently enough, you may be taken by surprise when vehicles come past. The first time you spot a vehicle it may be a tiny speck. The next time it may almost be on top of you.

Many drivers get very close to the vehicle in front just before overtaking. This can frighten the driver in front and increase the risk of an accident. Then, when they do move out, drivers often overtake too

Overtaking

Because of the mixture of traffic, the skill of overtaking is essential. You will not want to follow a convoy of lorries slowly climbing a hill.

The rules about overtaking on motorways are the same as for other roads. So where is the problem? Unless you scan the traffic pattern ahead constantly, you may not realise how rapidly you are closing in on the vehicle ahead. You also need to be aware of what is happening

– Once you have seen it's safe to go past, overtake quickly to avoid 'boxing in'.

slowly. This boxes in the driver being overtaken for much longer than is necessary or safe.

It is safest to start overtaking while you are still at least two seconds behind the driver in front. Make sure it is safe, and then move into the next lane. Once you have moved out, and seen that it is safe to go past, accelerate. Overtake quickly. Try to spend the least amount of time possible in a position that boxes in the driver being overtaken.

Drivers catch up with slow-moving traffic quickly, suddenly realise the need to move out and, without really looking, start to change lane. They signal halfway into the next lane and just hope that there is no one overtaking them. Watch for situations like this. Consider using a long headlight flash (several seconds) before passing. (See the panel on this subject below.)

Make sure the driver(s) of the vehicle(s) you are about to overtake know you are there. Do this while you are still at least two seconds away. Make sure they are holding a steady speed and position before you overtake. If, on the other hand,

you are about to pull out and you see a driver coming up flashing their lights, don't immediately pull out. Wait. If they appear to be holding back to let you out, then gently move out. Keep checking, just in case you have misinterpreted the signal. Many accidents on motorways are 'shunts'. These occur when a driver suddenly pulls out to overtake without seeing a vehicle about to overtake him, whose driver didn't believe the slower vehicle would move out into his path.

Where traffic merges, for example at a junction or where two motorways merge, there may be a lot of hasty and misjudged lane changing by vehicles joining or leaving the motorway.

As far as possible, you are best to avoid overtaking at junctions. It is much safer to let the traffic pattern settle again first.

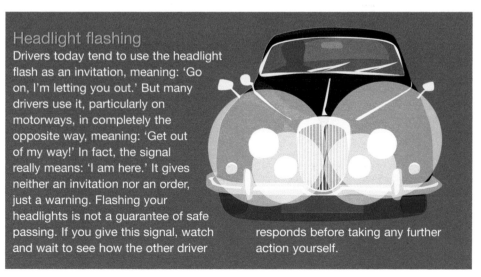

Headlight flashing

Drivers today tend to use the headlight flash as an invitation, meaning: 'Go on, I'm letting you out.' But many drivers use it, particularly on motorways, in completely the opposite way, meaning: 'Get out of my way!' In fact, the signal really means: 'I am here.' It gives neither an invitation nor an order, just a warning. Flashing your headlights is not a guarantee of safe passing. If you give this signal, watch and wait to see how the other driver responds before taking any further action yourself.

Unless you like playing sardines, there is another problem for you to consider. Imagine that you are driving along in the middle lane. You have a lorry directly to your left and a car to your right. You are all doing the same speed. You are the sardine in the sandwich and you have no escape if either of the other drivers moves to the middle lane. You cannot rely on drivers to check properly before they move.

Try to time your arrival alongside the car or the lorry so that the vehicle in the right-hand lane has either already passed you, or is still a little way behind you. In other words, keep a space on one side of you. Always avoid driving three abreast.

Even if the other drivers do look, they may not see you because – if you're alongside them – you are likely to be in their blindspot. Try not to drive in someone else's blindspot. Either get slightly ahead so that they can see you out front, or stay back to be visible in their mirrors.

After overtaking, drivers frequently misjudge and cut in on the vehicle they have overtaken. To avoid this problem it is best to wait and watch for the vehicle you are overtaking to appear in your interior mirror and not in the misleading convex door mirror that makes the vehicle look further away than it really is. This normally ensures that you go far enough past before moving back.

– Driving three-abreast in a 'sardine sandwich' is dangerous because it reduces your options.

– Never forget that you are not allowed to reverse if you miss your exit, not even along the hard shoulder.

To summarise, you should aim to overtake quickly and safely, and to move back in as soon as you safely can. You should:

– Anticipate where other drivers may change lanes

– Avoid the 'sandwich' situation of driving three abreast

– Try not to drive in someone else's blindspot

– Use the interior mirror, rather than the door mirror, to help you judge when to move back in.

Leaving a motorway

Unless you are going to the end of the motorway, you will need to leave by one of the exits. These are all numbered. When you plan your route, make a note of the exit number for the junction you intend using. The signs on the motorway are designed to be read from some distance because of the higher driving speeds involved. This means there is only space on the sign to put the main destinations and route numbers; your destination may not even be mentioned. Also, some larger towns and cities may be served by several exits.

By checking a map before you set out you can find the most convenient one for you. Unless you know the exit number, it's very easy to miss your turn off or end up taking a less direct route.

Never forget that you are not allowed to reverse if you miss your exit, not even along the hard shoulder. You must go on to another exit and find a way to rejoin your route.

You need to look well ahead for signs telling you of junctions. The first sign will be a mile from the exit. Bear in mind that signs can be obscured by high-sided vehicles, especially if you are driving in the middle or right-hand lane.

Drivers sometimes leave it late to exit the motorway and may cut across lanes of traffic to reach their junction, even at the last minute. Expect this and keep well

177

– When leaving the motorway, check your speedometer on the deceleration lane.

clear of other drivers. Aim to be in the left-hand lane at about the half-mile sign.

Traffic in the left-hand lane may be moving faster, so there may be drivers overtaking you on your left.

Glance to the left before changing lane. Signal and only move when there is a safe gap. Once in the left-hand lane, give an early signal that you intend to leave the motorway. Do this between the 300- and 200-metre markers.

Traffic around you may leave without warning at any time, so keep a look out for traffic passing you to leave at the same exit.

Some drivers illegally use the hard shoulder to get past traffic on the inside and reach the exit sooner. Before moving into the deceleration lane, make a quick shoulder check, just in case someone is passing you on the hard shoulder. They shouldn't… but they might.

Keep your speed consistent until you reach the deceleration lane. This helps reduce the risk of traffic bunching up.

Remember, speed deceives. You will be travelling faster than you think. Deceleration lanes head into slip roads which often contain sharp bends. Many accidents occur on slip roads because drivers are still going too fast. Check your speedometer so that you know your speed. Look well ahead for any signs warning you of sharp bends and speed limits. Use your brakes good and early and check your speed again. The speed limits shown are designed to keep you on the road, not to slow your journey.

The slip road can be quite short, so the junction may come up much faster than you expect. A queue of traffic may be stationary ahead. If the slip road runs downhill as well, it can make stopping even more difficult, especially in the wet.

– Many accidents occur on slip roads because drivers are still going too fast.

Make sure you can stop at the junction if you need to. Brake early and gently on the deceleration lane; others behind may have misjudged their speed. Having left the motorway, give your senses a chance to readjust to the speeds of ordinary roads. This is a good time for a break in your journey.

To recap, your main aim is to make a smooth, well-planned exit from the motorway:

– Know the number of the exit you want to take in advance

– Look well ahead for warning signs

– Be in the left-hand lane by about the half-mile sign

– Watch out for drivers leaving at the last minute

– Give a signal between the 300- and 200-metre countdown markers

– Make a quick shoulder check before moving into the deceleration lane

– Speed deceives – check your speedometer, brake early and keep to the posted speed limits

– Make sure you can stop at the junction if you need to

– Give your senses a chance to readjust to the speeds you will encounter on ordinary roads.

Night driving on motorways

Driving at night on an unlit motorway can be very disorientating. The normal clues you use to gauge position and speed aren't there. Visibility may be restricted to your headlight beams. Only the lights of other vehicles, their size and brightness, help you to establish your position and speed. And with so little to look at, staying awake can be difficult.

You can use the coloured studs to help orientate yourself in poor visibility or at night. The red studs change to green studs at exits and entrances. This helps you to find exits for leaving the motorway and to know when drivers are likely to be joining. The studs help you to stay in your lane.

Not everyone has good night vision. Some people have what is called night blindness. This can be detected during an eyesight test. If you find night driving a strain, schedule your journey so that you can finish in daylight.

You must use headlights after lighting-up time – lighting-up time is between dusk and dawn – on all motorways, even if they are lit. Use dipped headlights:

– Whenever main beam might dazzle oncoming drivers on the opposite carriageway

– When following other vehicles.

Make sure your headlight beam does not shine inside the car in front.

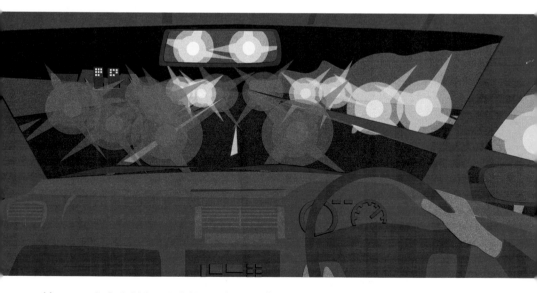

– Many people find driving at night on a busy, unlit motorway very disorienting.

Bad weather

Bad weather only adds to the problems. Drivers still hurry and still take risks. Seeing is difficult, and so is stopping when you do see the danger. Drivers lose control, lorries skid sideways and throw up spray. Many drivers still won't switch on their lights, and drive too fast and too close. The bad weather isn't to blame for accidents – it merely exposes the poor standard of driving skill. You need to allow more time for your journey.

In high winds, high-sided vehicles may get blown over in front of you. Slow down, and beware when driving on exposed stretches of road.

– In wet weather, remember that lorries throw up a lot of spray and can temporarily reduce your visibility to virtually zero.

If it is windy, it can affect your steering, especially if the wind is coming from the left. As you pass a large vehicle or come out from under a bridge, you can be pushed to the right by a sudden gust of wind. This can feel very alarming and your best bet is to slow down.

Drivers find it difficult to see or be seen in bad weather. Put on your dipped headlights whenever conditions worsen. If you need to use the wipers, you need your lights. Make sure other drivers can see you.

You must use your headlights or front fog lights when visibility is seriously reduced, that is when you cannot see for more than 100 metres. Do not use your rear fog lights unless visibility is reduced to less than 100 metres.

Studies have shown that no particular colour of car gives a real advantage in a range of conditions. In all cases, the use of lights means being seen more easily, and correctly adjusted, dipped headlights do not dazzle other drivers. Contrary to popular belief, driving with your lights on does not drain the battery; while the engine is running the battery is being recharged.

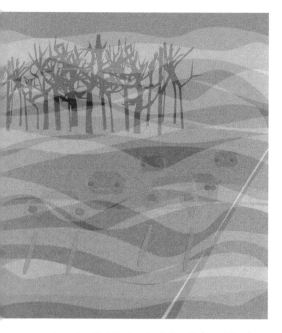

– Imagine that just out of view beyond the fog is a stationary queue of vehicles.

you can stop in that distance. For 20 metres visibility you should be going no faster than 20mph. For 30 metres – 30mph. This is a reasonable rule of thumb: one metre of visibility equals a maximum of 1mph of speed.

Even in bad weather, drivers travel much too close together. Increase the gap between you and the vehicle in front so that you can pull up safely if it suddenly slows down or stops.

Use the guide given in section 11, 'Following at a safe distance'. Use the two-second rule, but in bad weather increase this to at least three seconds.

You cannot rely on other drivers staying where they are. Only overtake if really necessary. Spend as little time as possible alongside another driver. Driving in bad weather is very tiring, especially at night. Most importantly, take regular breaks. If your journey isn't necessary, don't start out. Whatever you do, allow more time for your journey.

Despite poor weather conditions, drivers still hurry and try to make up time when late. Slow down – accept that your journey will take longer. If you can, telephone ahead and explain why you are delayed, but never use a handheld mobile phone while driving.

Never drive so fast that you cannot stop well within the distance you can see to be clear. You need to imagine that just out of view beyond the fog is a standing queue of vehicles in all the lanes. How do you know there isn't? So, if you can only see 20 metres in front of you, make sure

Rules to remember:

– Lights on

– Slow down

– Increase the gap

– Take regular breaks.

Accidents

Most accidents on motorways are caused by drivers following too closely and/or driving too fast for the conditions. Watch for slow-moving or stationary traffic ahead – an accident may have just occurred. Watch for the flashing lights of emergency vehicles.

If you do witness an accident, here are some things that you should and should not do.

If the accident is on the other carriageway either stop by an emergency telephone on the hard shoulder and give details. If you are not in a position to pull over, just concentrate on your driving. Don't rubberneck! Turning your head to stare at the incident with ghoulish curiosity may cause another accident because drivers become distracted.

If the accident is on your side, the same points apply. Switch on your hazard warning lights. This will help to warn following traffic of the problem ahead. Give help as far as you are able. Be alert to the danger of fire and dangerous chemicals. Don't smoke and don't let others smoke either.

It is better to use a roadside phone even if you have a car phone. The roadside phone automatically identifies where you are to the police in the control unit. This speeds up response, with a consequent saving of life.

– If the weather's bad and your journey isn't really necessary, don't start out.

Giving these details is important:

– Which carriageway the accident is on

– How many vehicles are involved

– Any hazardous chemicals (note the hazchem number)

– How many people are injured

– Whether the road is completely blocked.

Always remember, never walk on the motorway itself except in an emergency. It is not like crossing a normal road. Many people have been killed simply attempting to cross from the central reservation to the hard shoulder. Stay where you are, unless you are in danger. It is illegal to walk anywhere on the motorway except in an emergency.

Services on motorways

The service areas are usually next to the motorway. Most motorways have these at regular intervals. The range of services available varies, but most offer catering and fuel facilities. When you plan your route, make a note of the service areas you will pass. This will allow you to take convenient breaks. A 15-minute break, at least every two to three hours, will be welcomed by drivers and passengers.

Advance information signs, similar to the ones used for junctions, alert you to the next service area, and the same advice for exiting a motorway at a junction applies, including judging your speed. Take care when entering the service area: there will be people walking about,

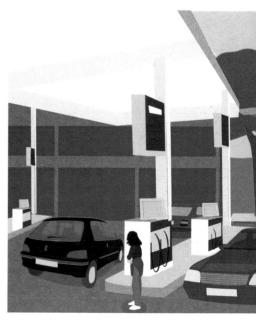

vehicles manoeuvring in and out of spaces, moving or stopping suddenly.

Slow right down. Speed limits may be signed. If not, you need to imagine a child may run out from anywhere. Keep your speed low enough to stop easily, particularly in the wet and at night. Use the stop as an opportunity to check over the car. On returning to the motorway, follow the advice given earlier about joining. Do allow some time to readjust again.

– Service areas provide a useful break from long motorway journeys, but remember to adjust your speed as you exit the motorway and watch out for people and parking cars.

Breakdowns

If you feel that something is wrong with your car, don't be tempted to push on. It is safer to choose to stop somewhere convenient, like the next services, the next exit or the next emergency telephone, rather than wait for the inevitable.

Use the nearest emergency telephone; they are normally either at one-mile or one-kilometre intervals. The marker posts along the hard shoulder show the direction to go to the nearest telephone. The telephone is a free connection to the police motorway control centre.

Take details with you of your car and membership of breakdown organisations

– Never attempt to retrieve something that may have fallen from your vehicle.

you subscribe to. If you don't have membership, the police can arrange for a local breakdown service to come out. The cost of this service can be high and must be met by you. Wait for assistance by your car – but not inside your vehicle. If the phone doesn't work a police patrol will stop and help. They make special runs along sections where the phones aren't working.

If something has fallen from your car, use the same basic procedure. Do not attempt to retrieve it yourself.

If you are a woman travelling alone, state this to the police when you phone. You will normally get priority. When you return to your car, leave the passenger door open so that you can get back in if anyone other than the police or breakdown organisation stops. Once inside lock all the doors. You can buy signs that ask passing drivers to 'phone police'.

Some breakdowns affect the control of your car. For example, if your nearside front tyre bursts you should hold the steering wheel firmly to keep the car in a straight line – it will tend to pull to the left – while you check to see when you can change lanes. Don't brake – the brakes won't be able to slow a wheel with a deflated tyre. If the left front tyre bursts, braking will tend to make the car pull to the right. When you can see a gap in the traffic, signal and – steering very gently – move across to the hard shoulder and let the car roll to a stop on the hard shoulder. Come to rest as far to the left as you can, while leaving room for work to be done on the wheel.

Switch on your hazard warning lights, if fitted. Then get out of the nearside door. It is usually safer to get everyone out of the car, and to sit on the bank well away from the carriageway. Unfortunately, many accidents occur involving vehicles on the hard shoulder.

Staying alert

Drivers frequently fall asleep at the wheel. When you drive on a motorway you are likely to find that you get very bored.

– Fresh air and regular breaks can help avoid the onset of highway hypnosis.

You may mentally 'switch off' and develop the blank stare known as 'highway hypnosis'. This is more likely to occur at night and will only be made worse if you are tired already, although it can easily happen in daylight as well.

Make sure that you are fit to drive before you start. This means well rested, and not too tense. If someone else can do or share the driving, let them.

Make use of the car's ventilation to help keep you alert. Take breaks as often as you need to. Ask yourself while you are driving: 'Am I concentrating?' If you find it difficult to keep your eyes moving, have a break.

If you have been drinking alcohol, don't drive. It slows down your reactions and makes judging speed and distance even harder.

Ignorance

Do you know the rules? Do other drivers know the rules? Here's an example. When you are driving along, you may see a lorry with the letters TIR on the back, usually somewhere above the number plate. Do you know what it means? Do you need to know?

TIR means Transport International Routiers and should cause you to exercise extra caution when you see it on one of those large lorries. TIR is used when goods are transported on international routes crossing many borders. More and

– BSM have campaigned for years to make motorway driving part of the driving test.

more drivers travel across Europe, and they may come from other countries and be used to different rules.

Don't expect TIR lorry drivers to behave according to the rules. Even if they know they shouldn't overtake on the left unless traffic is moving in queues, they may choose to ignore the rule. Besides, this rule doesn't apply in some countries and the driver may not know our rules.

End of motorway regulations

So there ends so many pages about motorways. Why so many?

First, because motorway driving is not part of the driving test, even though commonsense dictates that it should be. BSM has campaigned for many years to get this changed, as indeed have most organisations concerned with road safety.

Second, because only a relatively small percentage of people bother to receive any formal training on motorway driving. These pages do attempt to provide you with a good idea of what will be involved and how to stay out of trouble. But they cannot be a substitute for a structured motorway driving session with an Approved Driving Instrctor.

BSM has also introduced a motorway programme for their driving simulators. The two-hour programme is designed to provide new drivers with a realistic introduction to motorway driving. It allows you to practise joining the motorway, keeping the right distance away from other traffic, overtaking and leaving the motorway. You also have the chance to drive in rain and fog as well as negotiating motorway roadworks and driving at night time.

Third, because although you learnt some or all of the rules and procedures in order to pass your Driving Theory Test, that may have been some time ago, and rules are quickly forgotten unless they are used in real life. Ignorance can kill, and the roads are certainly no exception.

If you wish to find out more about the motorway simulator course or taking a motorway lesson with a professional BSM instructor please contact your local BSM Centre on 08457 276 276.

Good luck!

Index